Responsible Leadership in Projects

Insights Into Ethical Decision Making

Findings from a Research Project Sponsored by the Project Management Institute
February 2017

Nicholas Clarke, PhD
Professor of Organisational Behaviour & HRM
EADA Business School
Barcelona, Spain

Alessia D'Amato, PhD
Lecturer in Organisational Behaviour & HRM
Southampton Business School
University of Southampton
Southampton, United Kingdom

Malcolm Higgs, PhD
Professor of Organisational Behaviour & HRM
Southampton Business School
University of Southampton
Southampton, United Kingdom

Ramesh Vahidi, PhD
Teaching Fellow in Project Management
Southampton Business School
University of Southampton
Southampton, United Kingdom

Library of Congress Cataloging-in-Publication Data

Names: Clarke, Nicholas, 1966- author. | Project Management Institute,
  issuing body.
Title: Responsible leadership in projects : insights into ethical decision
  making / findings from a research project sponsored by the Project
  Management Institute, February 2017 ; Nicholas Clarke [and three others].
Description: Newtown Square, Pennsylvania : Project Management Institute,
  Inc., [2018] | Includes bibliographical references.
Identifiers: LCCN 2017053637 (print) | LCCN 2017055621 (ebook) | ISBN
  9781628254778 (ePUB) | ISBN 9781628254785 (kindle) | ISBN 9781628254792
  (Web PDF) | ISBN 9781628254761 (pbk. : alk. paper)
Subjects: LCSH: Project management—Moral and ethical aspects. | Leadership.
  | Decision making.
Classification: LCC HD69.P75 (ebook) | LCC HD69.P75 C52223 2018 (print) | DDC
  658.4/092—dc23
LC record available at https://lccn.loc.gov/2017053637

ISBN: 978-1-62825-476-1

Published by: Project Management Institute, Inc.
          14 Campus Boulevard
          Newtown Square, Pennsylvania 19073-3299 USA
          Phone: +1 610-356-4600
          Fax: +1 610-482-9971
          Email: customercare@pmi.org
          Internet: PMI.org

To inquire about discounts for resale or educational purposes, please contact the PMI Book
Service Center.

          PMI Book Service Center
          P.O. Box 932683, Atlanta, GA 31193-2683 USA
          Phone: +1 866-276-4764 (within the U.S. or Canada) or
          + 1 770-280-4129 (globally)
          Fax: + 1 770-280-4113
          Email: info@bookorders.pmi.org

Printed in the United States of America. No part of this work may be reproduced or trans-
mitted in any form or by any means, electronic, manual, photocopying, recording, or by any
information storage and retrieval system, without prior written permission of the publisher.

The paper used in this book complies with the Permanent Paper Standard issued by the
National Information Standards Organization (Z39.48—1984).

                    10 9 8 7 6 5 4 3 2 1

Acknowledgments

We would like to express our gratitude to Dr. Henry Linger, PMI project liaison, and the Project Management Institute for funding this research.

Contents

CHAPTER 1

Executive Summary

Background

This is the first study to investigate how relationships among a project manager, team members, and stakeholders bring about ethical or personal conflicts for project managers (Aaltonen & Sivonen, 2009; Jepsen & Eskerod, 2009). This study also examines the impact of these relationships on ethical and social responsibility decision making. A literature is growing concerning the importance of Corporate Social Responsibility (CSR) considerations (Laschinger, Brent, & Claasen, 2005) as well as ethical issues for projects (Jonasson & Ingason, 2013). In addition, many project management textbooks as well as professional standards now contain sections relating to ethical practice (Schwalbe, 2011; Sears, Sears, & Clough, 2013). More recently, the significance of these topic areas has resulted in the Project Management Institute (PMI) funding research projects looking at project management and sustainability (Gareis, Huemann, Martinuzzi, Sedlacko, & Weninger, 2013) as well as reexamining new thinking in the area of stakeholder management (e.g., Eskerod, Huemann, & Ringhofer, 2015). The term *responsible leadership* has gained currency in the literature as denoting leadership that combines an emphasis on both ethical behaviors and social responsibility concerns (Maak & Pless, 2006a, 2006b).

To date, limited empirical research has been conducted examining responsible leadership in action, and we have only a shallow understanding of how managers' leadership actions interact with ethical judgments or CSR concerns (De Hoogh & Den Hartog, 2008; Pless, 2007), especially in the case of project management. There is reason to believe that projects might actually impose some constraints on this form of leadership. Most project managers learn that success is about delivering projects on time and on budget (Lock, 1987; Wright, 1997). Do the consensual solutions that represent the *sine qua non* of responsible leadership thus pose problems for traditional approaches to project management? Further, the use of cost-benefit analysis as a decision-making tool by project managers has been criticized because it fails to take into account ethical considerations (Van Wee, 2012). This study offers new and original insights on the nature of personal, value, and ethical dilemmas faced by project managers and the factors that influence how they make ethical or value-related decisions. Given the paucity of empirical research in the area of ethical decision making and responsible leadership, the findings from this study will have implications for leadership in projects and ethical decision making more widely.

The Study

We conducted a qualitative study and undertook semi-structured interviews with project team members and their stakeholders based in a major United Kingdom–based insurance business. The study was longitudinal and we collected data from four projects over the course of 12 months to gain a better understanding of the dynamic nature of decision-making processes and the contextual factors that influence them.

Key Findings

Although all four projects studied were found to deal with issues that have ethical or moral dimensions exemplified by value conflicts, project members tended not to see these issues as ethical ones. Cognitive models of decision making, such as the one put forward by Rest (1986), emphasize moral awareness as an essential first key step in the ethical decision-making process. Our findings, however, suggest that in organizational settings, these personal value conflicts are interpreted through the lens of the organization's culture and business priorities such that ethical issues are not explicitly seen as such.

How project members engage in ethical decision making does not fit well with a rationalist approach to understanding the ethical decision-making process. Rest (1986), for example, posits a four-step model of ethical decision making and behavior that characterizes ethical decision making as proceeding through four stages: (1) moral awareness, (2) moral judgment, (3) moral intent, and (4) moral behavior. Instead, our findings suggest that how project members viewed a moral dilemma shifted as time progressed and their interpretations of a situation varied as different events unfolded during the course of a project.

The moral intensity of an issue or problem was found to vary over time as project members interacted with different people and situations. These served as "trigger" events that resulted in project members interpreting or reinterpreting the moral dilemma in different ways. These trigger events were found to provoke cognitive dissonance, which resulted in a series of ongoing rationalizations or legitimization processes to justify the perspective of the situation taken. This suggests that ethical decision making is more akin to a sensemaking process in real-life organizational settings rather than a sequential, rational, cognitive analysis of a moral dilemma.

The organizational culture was found to play a significant role in this sensemaking process. This culture was characterized as being paternalistic and caring, although risk averse. A core value of this organization was "serving our members (customers)." This resulted in decision-making processes being driven by the need for consensus involving a number of stakeholders. Consensus building meant establishing shared mental models that influenced how project members interpreted moral issues in their projects.

Consensus building meant that high levels of stakeholder engagement and management were a distinctive aspect of the decision-making process in these projects. This led to greater accountability for decision making and the notion that decision making was shared or dispersed across a wide network of key actors. This played a significant role in shaping how project members interpreted ethical dilemmas and their subsequent actions.

History in terms of the relative success and experience of previous projects in the organization was a major lens through which project members made sense of and interpreted ethical issues and gave meaning to moral situations that arose on projects.

Ethical situations arose on projects where conflicts were experienced between project and organizational priorities and unclear boundaries of project members' roles and responsibilities. In these circumstances, the project's governance structure was used to help resolve ethical issues that arose. However, this could involve significant politicking and the selected lobbying of particular stakeholders in order to secure particular decision outcomes. This, again, suggests that ethical decision making was far less a cognitive, rational process than it was subject to actors persuading and cajoling powerful others to secure outcomes that supported their priorities.

Ethical decision making is a core aspect of responsible leadership, but rational approaches to ethical decision making suggest individuals will judge moral situations in terms of absolute moral standards or universal principles. Our findings suggest that ethical decision making in projects and organizations does not mirror this rationalistic perspective. Instead, ethical decision making is a dynamic process where individuals negotiate and make sense of moral situations through interactions with key stakeholders, and engage in a continuous process of interpretation and reinterpretation of the issue as events unfold. This sensemaking would seem highly dependent upon contextual factors in the organization, including the organizational culture.

Contributions to Theory

This study makes a contribution to the literatures on both ethical decision making and responsible leadership as well as to project management literature.

In many studies of ethical decision making, there is a focus on a normative approach to considerations of ethics rather than exploration as an enacted phenomenon. In reviewing the literature on ethical decision making, we found a focus on rational models (e.g., Jones, 1991; Rest, 1986). However, these have been critiqued as they fail to take account of the high levels of uncertainty and ambiguity that are faced in many contexts and the related emotional aspects of decisions. Sonenshein (2007) developed a model that takes account of these additional factors, adopting a sensemaking perspective (Weick, 1995). However, to date there have been relatively few empirical studies that have tested this approach. This study provides empirical data that provide support for the Sonenshein (2007) model and, in particular, shows that a sensemaking perspective (Weick, 1995) plays a significant role in the issue-construction component of the model.

In recent years, there has been growing attention to ethics studies in the project management literature (Müller, 2014). However, these studies have tended to be somewhat limited in scope and lack evidence of the practice behaviors of project managers (Loo, 2002; Müller, 2014; Walker & Lloyd-Walker, 2014). This study provides insights into the behavior and actions of both project managers and team members in the course of working on significant projects. Furthermore, the practices, behaviors, and ethical issues are studied on a longitudinal basis, demonstrating how the impacts of a range of factors on ethical issues and decisions play out over the course of the project.

Within the literature on ethical decision making and ethics in projects, there have been assertions that organizational culture is a factor that impacts decisions and behaviors (Ho, 2010; Sweeney, Arnold, & Pierce, 2010). However, there is limited empirical evidence underpinning these assertions. This study provides evidence of the central role that organizational culture plays in the ethical decision-making process and in resolving issues and dilemmas. Responsible leadership remains an emerging concept that suffers from definitional disagreements and a lack of guidance in terms of moving from theory to application in practice (Maak & Pless, 2006a; Voegtlin, 2015).

Within our study, we found evidence that responsible leadership plays a significant role in the practical context of managing complex and ambiguous projects. In particular, we have demonstrated that extensive stakeholder engagement plays a significant role in contributing to handling ethical issues and dilemmas.

Contributions to Practice

Given the paucity of empirical research in the area of ethical decision making and responsible leadership, the findings from this study will have implications for leadership in projects—and more widely. The outcomes of this research will enable PMI to consider in what ways ethical standards of practice meet the requirements for project management practice. Furthermore, the findings can inform the development of project managers by providing input that can develop awareness of how context and moral intensity might influence the decisions project managers make on projects.

The significance of a sensemaking approach to ethical decision making provides a basis for developing project managers' understanding of the sensemaking processes, thus enhancing their understanding of approaches to handling ethical dilemmas and decision making.

CHAPTER 2

Introduction

Within the project management literature, there has been an increasing interest in issues relating to ethics and ethical decision making (Aaltonen & Sivonen, 2009; Jepsen & Eskerod, 2009; Schwalbe, 2011; Sears, Sears, & Clough, 2013). However, to date there have been few empirical studies that consider how ethical considerations arise in projects and how issues are resolved by project team members and those in leadership roles within the project (De Hoogh & Den Hartog, 2008; Pless, 2007). Indeed, this will be the first study to investigate how relationships among project managers, team members, and stakeholders bring about ethical or personal conflicts for project managers—and to examine the impact of those relationships on ethical and social responsibility decision making. Furthermore, the project has been designed to explore how those with leadership roles in projects exercise their leadership in a way that addresses the growing need for ethical decision making in projects. In doing this, we explore the literature on responsible leadership and its evidence in the behaviors of leaders within this study. The concept of responsible leadership has gained currency in the literature, denoting leadership that combines an emphasis on both ethical behavior and social responsibility concerns (Maak & Pless, 2006a).

To date, limited empirical research has been conducted examining responsible leadership in action, and we have only a shallow understanding of how managers' leadership actions interact with ethical judgments or CSR concerns (De Hoogh & Den Hartog, 2008; Pless, 2007). This is also the case of project management.

This project commenced with a review of the literature relating to responsible leadership, ethics in project management, and ethical decision making. In performing this review, we identified a number of gaps in the existing research. There has been growing attention to ethics studies in project management literature in recent years (Müller, 2014). However, these studies have tended to be somewhat limited in scope and lack evidence of the practical behavior of project managers (Loo, 2002; Müller, 2014; Walker & Lloyd-Walker, 2014). Furthermore, many studies focus on a normative approach to considerations of ethics rather than exploring ethics as an enacted phenomenon. In reviewing the literature on ethical decision making, we found a focus on rational models (e.g., Jones, 1991; Rest, 1986). However, these have been critiqued as they fail to take account of the high levels of uncertainty and ambiguity that are faced in many contexts and the related emotional aspects of decisions. Sonenshein (2007) developed a model that takes account of these additional factors, adopting a sensemaking perspective (Weick, 1995). However, to date there have been relatively few empirical studies that have tested this approach.

The aims of this study were to investigate the enablers and constraints to responsible leadership in projects through exploring the ethical issues faced by project managers as they interact with project members and stakeholders. We aim to make a specific contribution to the literature by shedding new insights on project managers' perceptions of the moral intensity of personal and value conflicts they face on projects and how these impact their decision making. Our specific research questions were:

1. What personal value conflicts arise for project members on projects and what are the values or mind-sets that direct their decision making?

2. How do interactions with stakeholders reveal insights into ethical decision making on projects?

3. What are the norms that regulate how project members deal with personal conflicts in projects, and to what extent do they provide an ethical orientation for project managers?

In exploring these questions, we employed a phenomenological approach to map the interrelationships between personal conflicts, ethical issues, decision making, and their impact within four projects within the finance industry in the United Kingdom. Drawing upon a processual, in-depth case study approach (Yin, 2003), we analyzed the series of interpersonal interactions and ethical issues that arose among project managers, their team members, and stakeholders over the course of 12 months in four projects. All of the projects were located in the same organization, which provides an extensive range of domestic and commercial products, including vehicle, homeowners, and business insurance; pensions; and investments. The four projects were analyzed individually, followed by a cross-case analysis (Yin, 2003).

Overall, this study will offer new and original insights into the nature of personal, value, and ethical dilemmas faced by project managers and the factors that influence how they make ethical or value-related decisions, along with the role that leadership plays in this context. Given the paucity of empirical research in the area of ethical decision making and responsible leadership, the findings from this study will have implications for leadership in projects and more widely. The outcomes of this research will enable PMI to consider in what ways ethical standards of practice meet the requirements for project management practice. Project managers will be more aware of how context and moral intensity might influence the decisions they make on projects.

The remainder of this report is organized as follows:

Chapters 3 to 5 provide a review of the three strands of literature that underpin our study (i.e., Responsible

Leadership, Ethics in Project Management, and Ethical Decision Making).

Chapters 6 describes the design of the research project and our approach to the analyses of the data.

Chapter 7 provides detailed descriptions of the findings within each of the four individual project case studies.

Chapter 8 discusses the findings and analysis of the four cases in light of the literature relating to ethics and responsible leadership.

Chapter 9 summarizes our key findings and conclusions, and outlines the contributions of the study to both theory and practice, together with our comments on the research limitations.

CHAPTER 3

Responsible Leadership

The practice of leadership compels business organizations to pay attention to the impact of their operations on society, as companies are social enterprises and therefore responsible to society at large (Amaladoss & Manohar, 2013). This view of leadership is combined with recent calls for a new form of leadership in conducting business that addresses the diverse economic, social, and environmental issues that the globalization process has created. Other writers point toward the need to transcend neo-economic instrumentalism, one of the main factors that gave rise to the collapse in financial markets and the retrenchment and stagnation across many of the world's economies (Maak & Pless, 2006b; Scherer & Palazzo, 2008).

Against this backdrop, the concept of responsible leadership has emerged, seeking to bring together notions of leadership, ethics, and corporate social responsibility to underpin a new form of leadership that is better suited to the changing nature of global business and the challenges it brings (Doh & Stumpf, 2005; Waldman & Siegel, 2008). A poll conducted in France, Germany, Great Britain, Italy, Spain, and the United States in 2009 found that 76% of Americans, and between 65% and 81% of European adults, considered the behavior of their business leaders unethical or irresponsible (Harris Interactive, 2009). Therefore, there is growing awareness of the need for a new form of leadership where social responsibility and ethical behaviors are increasingly central to the exercise of leadership (Carroll & Shabana, 2010), and that reflects a step change in the social contract between society and business.

Conceptualizing Responsible Leadership: A Glance Across the Literature

Responsible leadership considers the implications of an increasingly complex and uncertain global business environment and compels business organizations to pay more attention to the impact that their operations have on the environment and ecosystem (Voegtlin, 2015; Voegtlin, Patzer, & Scherer, 2012). Conceptually, responsible leadership is understood by its proponents as an emerging concept at the intersection between ethics and leadership (Ciulla, 2005; Waldman & Siegel, 2008), but there is no consensus yet on either the foundation of the concept or the correlates in terms of antecedents and outcomes.

Although the field is only just emerging, most writers agree that responsible leadership requires a focus on leadership ethics and a more comprehensive engagement with the full range of stakeholders affected by business in order to develop more socially responsible leadership behavior (De Hoogh & Den Hartog, 2008; Maak, 2007; Maak & Pless, 2006a; Waldman & Galvin, 2008; Waldman & Siegel, 2008). This also means that the first way to classify the literature on responsible leadership systematically is alongside two interrelated dimensions: the degree of stakeholders' inclusion and the scope of responsibility.

The degree of stakeholder inclusion defines the degree to which the notion of responsible leadership comprises different sets of stakeholders, or, as in Savage, Timothy, Whitehead, and Blair (1991), a framework to evaluate the potential of different stakeholders. The second dimension describes the bandwidth of diverse types of responsibilities. The first perspective emerged from an eclectic reflection on the role of business leaders, and is based on contrasting the shareholder orientation of business leaders with a broader stakeholder perspective (cf. Doh & Quigley, 2014; Freeman, 1984; Waldman & Galvin, 2008). Based on stakeholder theory, models have emerged to provide recommendations and guidance for stakeholder management (Mitchell, Agle, & Wood, 1997; Savage et al., 1991).

One of the most representative models is the conceptualization of responsible leadership by Maak and Pless (2006a, 2006b). This identifies the foundation of the concept of responsible leadership in a stakeholder society, and highlights the social-relational and ethical dimensions. Responsible leadership is the "art of building and sustaining good relationships with all the relevant stakeholders" (Maak & Pless, 2006a, p. 40); however, the idea of building and sustaining good relationships does not always reflect goodwill actions toward sustainability. Maak and Pless (2006b) developed a model discussing the qualitative roles of responsible leaders who act as citizens, stewards, servants, and visionaries. Responsible leaders are like weavers whose strength lies in the ties that bind stakeholders together (Maak & Pless, 2006a, p. 25). This also means that they will lead from the center, focusing on relationship building rather than power development. In addition, the more operational roles of architect, change agent, coach, and storyteller are discussed in this framework.

The core of the model suggests that the responsible leader fulfils a multitude of integrated roles and becomes a coordinator, providing benefits not just for the organization but for all the stakeholders involved. The visionary role depicts future thinking among stakeholders; the steward role is the defender of relevant resources; and the servant role describes undertaking acts of citizenship for the community at large. The second set of roles includes storyteller, enabler, coach, architect, and change agent. Extending out from these roles are the stakeholders. The concept of responsible leadership, as theorized in this model, aims to show the power of building relationships to enhance both performance and citizenship. This means that the relationships are at the center, over the individual person. This also reinforces the concept of informal leadership: Although these leaders may not formally be in charge of decision-making processes, their role in decision making is critical (Stone-Johnson, 2014).

This model can be particularly effective to explain project management and the decision-making processes that involve different stakeholders in different moments. In project management, relations and shared leadership in the team and within the larger stakeholder group is critical. However, Voegtlin, Patzer, and Scherer (2012) have taken a different approach in thinking about responsible leadership. Their starting point is how theory and practice are struggling to re-conceptualize the role of corporations and their leaders as they seek to address the surge of public concern that has arisen from the recent financial crisis (Scherer & Palazzo, 2008; Waldman & Siegel, 2008). They also point to the need to focus on the causes and implications of current leadership challenges, which are rooted in the economic and moral dilemmas facing organizations. This means simultaneously considering individual actions and how firms are embedded within societal practices. Their conceptualization of responsible leadership draws on deliberative practices and discursive conflict resolution, a combination of a macro-view of the business as a political actor and a micro-view of leadership. In their theorization, the concept of responsible leadership tries to answer the question: "Who is responsible for what and toward whom in an interconnected business world?" (Voegtlin et al., 2012, p. 2). Therefore, responsible leadership is understood as the characteristic of leaders who are responsible for sustainability in their firms and in society, in an interconnected business world. This means considering the pluralistic and multifaceted tasks that leaders have to deal with and requires leaders to recognize moral problems in their decision-making process. Leaders need to use their influence for conflict resolution and need to invite stakeholders to join the discourse—working toward achieving consensus among participants. In this perspective, responsible leadership can be depicted as a continuum, ranging from non-responsible leadership (e.g., self-interested, egoistic leadership behavior acting on an instrumental rationale) to fully responsible leadership (e.g., based on discourse ethics and deliberation).

Maak and Pless's (2006a, 2006b) major contribution was to develop a model of roles of responsible leadership, while Voegtlin et al. (2012) offered a philosophical foundation and theoretical background for responsible leadership (e.g., how responsible leaders can address the challenges of globalization and the outcomes of responsible leadership). However, questions about what the catalysts and drivers of sustainability and the components of responsible leadership are remain largely unanswered. Doh and Stumpf (2005) suggest that responsible leadership and governance include three critical components: values-based leadership, ethical decision making, and high-quality stakeholder relationships. Responsible leadership is, again, an inclusive concept; this means that employees perceive their organizations as having an ethical and proactive stakeholder perspective toward stakeholders, including the employees themselves (Doh, Stumpf, & Tymon, 2011).

Hill and Jones (1992) propose stakeholder-agency theory to explain the characteristics of the contractual relationships between a firm and its stakeholders, and to explain how business leaders seek to reconcile various stakeholders' interests. This perspective focuses on how business leaders affect the various social systems that both they and their companies are part of (Komives & Dugan, 2010; Miska, Stahl, & Medenhall, 2013). This means moving beyond a focus on individual- and organizational-level changes to collective leadership that relies on the strength of relationships among different stakeholders to foster and sustain change (Stone-Johnson, 2014). Furthermore, it attempts to bridge the individual level of leadership practice with the organizational level of corporate responsibility (Voegtlin et al., 2012). Maak and Pless (2006a) define responsible leadership as "a social-relational and ethical phenomenon, which occurs in social processes of interaction" (p. 99).

Moving Forward: From Theory to Practice

Because responsible leadership is not the same concept to everyone (Waldman & Galvin, 2008), scholars have suggested different practices that arise from various normative, descriptive, and paradigmatic points of view (Pless & Maak, 2011). From a normative perspective, authors call for an extended responsibility of organizations as a result of the globalization process posing new challenges to business and firms (Matten & Crane, 2005; Voegtlin, 2011). The normative perspective should enable leaders to act ethically by guiding leaders in establishing accepted norms and values through stakeholder dialogue. This intertwines with the debated concept of CSR (Carroll, 1999; D'Amato & Roome, 2009). Pless, Maak, and Waldman (2012), in their study based on interviews with business leaders, found marked differences in leaders' attitudes toward corporate social responsibility, which they termed their responsible orientation.

Based on rational egoism theory, Miska et al. (2013) display a mathematical model of responsible leaders that considers different types of incentives for stakeholder management. Rational egoism is the moral code that business leaders apply when pursuing long-term success. Its premise is the maximization of one's own good and self-interest (Woiceshyn, 2011). Although controversial, this does not have a cynical intent or a self-serving interest, but rather the recognition of reason as the ultimate source of knowledge and values and the only guide to action (Peikoff, 1991). This assumption is compatible with a common sense of ethics as it provides a guide for conducting business without harming others and is compatible with the agent, stakeholder, and converging views on responsible leadership (Miska et al., 2013). In this model, differing reasons for stakeholder engagement are considered and two perspectives included: the underlying perspective of responsible leadership and the implied degree of stakeholder inclusion and scopes of responsibility.

In this formula, "incentives" for stakeholder engagement are at the foundation, where the "incentives" refer to their discretionary nature (Carroll & Shabana, 2010) or the involvement. Two broad categories of such incentives define the mathematical model: (1) monetary and instrumental incentives, and (2) nonmonetary and noninstrumental incentives. Monetary and instrumental incentives for stakeholder engagement variably contribute to a company's economic returns; nonmonetary and noninstrumental incentives correspond to the ethical foundations of the stakeholder views and, in addition to economic goals, target societal and environmental responsibilities.

Three mainstream categories define the nature of the monetary and instrumental incentives: the strategic considerations, the anticipated negative costs and sanctions, and the societal expectations. Strategic considerations consider how responsible leadership can benefit a company's reputation positively, help attract and retain talent more easily, or justify premium prices for products (Miska et al., 2013; Waldman & Siegel, 2008). Anticipated negative costs and sanctions are more in line with the literature on irresponsible leadership (Bansal & Kandola, 2003; Cialdini & Goldstein, 2004). Finally, societal expectations would be factors such as societal activism that might lead to severe consequences for business leaders and their companies.

Examples of nonmonetary and noninstrumental incentives for stakeholder engagement include those that go beyond economic responsibilities and target societal and environmental goals (e.g., business leaders' values and authenticity, sense of care and duty to help, and personal corporate citizenship). The streamlined model describes a comprehensive structure that (1) allows incorporating business leaders' deliberations and considerations in accordance with the theory of rational egoism, and (2) is capable of reflecting how the two types of incentives for stakeholder engagement interact. This mathematical model of responsible leadership provides various examples based on rational consider-ations and explains the underlying decision-making mechanism. The overall intent was to show that it is possible to reconcile these facets and to go beyond the classical stakeholder–stockholder di-chotomy, although the major merit of this model is probably the attempt to systematically map the available "incentives." Another stream of research has shown the strategies for business leaders to acquire insights into their social responsibility when they en-gage in social partnership projects (Austin, 2006).

Conclusions

In conclusion, there are two main streams of research on re-sponsible leadership: the stakeholder view of responsible lead-ership (Maak & Pless, 2006a; Waldman & Balven, 2014) and the strategic/economic view (McWilliams & Siegel, 2001). Both viewpoints are integral to sustainable corporate responsibility (Pearce, Wassenaar, & Manz, 2014). This means that responsible leadership is balancing the need for immediate economic via-bility with the long-term benefits of stakeholders' participation and engagement. Shared leadership is also important. Shared leadership encourages responsibility at the core of the influence process through spreading leadership throughout the workforce (Pearce et al., 2014). This does not mean having to prefer shared leadership to hierarchical leadership, as these two are not mu-tually exclusive but rather work in tandem (Waldman & Balven, 2014). All of these three processes are intertwined and represent the foundation of project management: stakeholder engagement, the strategic view, and shared leadership. Overall, frameworks of responsible business leadership provide a useful lens to decipher ethics and the practice of project management.

CHAPTER 4

Ethics in Project Management

Introduction and Background

The modern business world is no stranger to various types of scandals here and there, many originating from ethical issues (see, for example, Gray & Larson, 2011; Jonasson & Ingason, 2013; Müller et al., 2013) and how those issues have been dealt with by the involved agents. Indeed, many of these scandals have happened in project environments (Müller, 2014) or could be, explicitly or implicitly, associated with projects in organizations. For instance, deficiencies and negligence in an original design project in car manufacturing might lead to later disasters in the production and operational phases. With the increasing dependence of the world's economy on projects and the rapid growth in the use of projects as a means for managing organizations (Bredillet, 2014; Frame, 2002; Lee, 2009; Turner, 2014; Turner, Huemann, Anbari, & Bredillet, 2010), paying due attention to ethical aspects to avoid any level of malpractice has become more significant (Bredillet, 2014; Jonasson & Ingason, 2013).

Pinto et al. (1998, cited in Lee, 2009) emphasize the importance of ethical skills in project management and for project managers because of their inevitable involvement in dealing with circumstances characterized by rapid change and uncertainties. These are linked to the potential for moral decision-making situations, as under such circumstances, project teams might feel they are under pressure to make the project successful and so will do "whatever it takes" (Lee, 2009, p. 460). It is also claimed by Pinto et al. that "Ethical behavior is often the first thing compromised in a high-risk environment" (Pinto et al., 1998, cited in Lee, p. 460).

Recent years have seen growing attention to ethics studies in project management (Müller, 2014). However, this has not been reflected in many of the popular project management textbooks (Loo, 2002; Müller, 2014; Walker & Lloyd-Walker, 2014). If the topic does appear in the text, it most likely does not receive the breadth and depth of coverage that it should/could. Initiation of more focused studies on the subject is associated with the research work by Norwegian scholars Erling Andersen and Ralf Müller and their further joint studies with an Australian group of researchers on the relations between ethics and governance (Müller, 2014).

In most of the reviewed key literature on ethics in project management, ethics is defined as an important subject either on its own or in relation to one or more areas, such as leadership (e.g., Gray & Larson, 2011; Kleim, 2004; Lee, 2009; Meredith & Mantel, 2009); risk (e.g., Nicolò, 1996); success (e.g., Jonasson & Ingason, 2013); governance and trust (e.g., Müller et al., 2013; Müller, Turner, Andersen, Shao, & Kvalnes, 2014; Turner, 2014); education (e.g., Helgado´ttir, 2008; Loo, 2002); human resource management and people in project-based organizations (e.g., Turner, 2014; Turner, Huemann, & Keegan, 2008); corporate culture (Cleland & Ireland, 2007; Kerzner, 2013); sustainability (e.g., Turner, 2014); and stakeholders (Eskerod, Huemann, & Ringhofer, 2015).

Nevertheless, Helgado´ttir (2008) posited a more comprehensive notion: ethics as one of the three pillars and core skills of modern project management, the other two being creative thinking and logical thinking. In this view, ethics is perceived as an overarching concept and skill rather than being limited to a set of tasks or standards with clearly defined and specific applications in one or a few areas of project management. Criticizing the retraining perspectives on ethics in the project management context, Jonasson and Ingason (2013) also dispute that it must be acknowledged as "a constant and limitless concept that should infuse, inspire, instigate and influence all of what we think and do as a professional" (p. 3). These thoughts are in line with the Aristotelian-based framework that Bredillet (2014) elaborates in his comprehensive discussion of the impact of ethics on project management theories and practice.

This chapter initially reviews the project management literature for definitions and concepts of ethics and the project management contexts in which these are discussed. This theoretical outline will be supplemented by discussing categories of ethical theories addressed in the relevant literature. Next, we provide insights into definitions of ethical dilemmas in projects, providing some examples from the literature. The trends and gaps based on recent and key publications are then discussed. Finally, the position and contributions of the current study and its alignment with the recent trends conclude this chapter.

Overview of Ethics Concept and Contexts in Project Management Academic Literature

There are various opinions on the extent and sufficiency of academic studies on "ethics" in the project management field. Reviewing the recent literature suggests that the disparity could be associated with the differences between what the authors mean by project ethics or ethics in project management, and what each of these encompasses (e.g., Bredillet, 2014; Jonasson & Ingason, 2013; Loo, 2002; Walker & Lloyd-Walker, 2014, to name a few). Although much has been published on or around the idea of a code of professional conduct in project management, the scarcity of fundamental academic studies on ethics in project management is repeatedly addressed in the literature (e.g., Loo, 2002; Müller, 2014; Müller et al., 2013; Walker & Lloyd-Walker, 2014). This is further exacerbated by the acknowledged differences between diverse perspectives on project management theory, more specifically.

A rather subjective and general definition of ethics by Jonasson and Ingason (2013) suggests that ethics deals with "what is good and just" and how people interact with one another in society (p. 7). Müller (2014) provides a more deliberate and sophisticated definition of ethics. He distinguishes between morals and ethics, associating morals with longitudinal development of "traditions and beliefs" on "right or wrong" doings, which informs people's "ethical reasoning process" in circumstances they face in projects (Müller, 2014).

Maylor (2010) names ethics as one of the main constraints on his model of a project, though he does not go beyond few words in defining its implications. Kerzner (2013) briefly discusses morality and ethics in the context of corporate culture, supplemented by several instances of ethical situations that a project manager might face. Although he occasionally refers to the benefits of companies defining codes of conduct and specially refers to the PMI Code of Ethics and Professional Conduct, the discussions do not go into depth drawing from the ethics theories in order to develop a theory or link these to the wider context of ethics in general. Cleland and Ireland (2007) also have a brief description of ethics as a "cultural element" in project management and similarly introduce the professional code of conduct from the American Society for the Advancement of Project Management (ASAPM).

These authors and many others that briefly and generally address the subject hardly provide an analytical or prescriptive view on the ways to approach projects' ethical issues, especially in the kinds of cases that Gray and Larson (2011) refer to as "gray areas of judgment and interpretation" (p. 355).

Gray and Larson (2011) consider ethics one of the aspects of "leading by example," with other aspects being priorities, urgency, problem solving, cooperation, and standards of performance.

They argue that project team members will (invariably) follow in the footsteps of or imitate the project manager's reactions to ethical situations when they face the same or similar issues. This originates from the fact that project managers' reactions are perceived as *acceptable behavior* (Gray & Larson, 2011); a similar viewpoint has been emphasized by Müller et al. (2013) and reiterated by Walker and Lloyd-Walker (2014).

Lee (2009), too, discusses ethics in a project leadership context, though she emphasizes the leadership of "virtual project teams" and their specific concerns, such as protecting privacy. She frequently draws from Kleim (2004), who links ethics to leadership, as well as highlights the interrelations among ethics, trust, and integrity. Kleim (2004) defines ethics as "adhering to values that determine the right decision or action" (p. 175), claiming that the project managers' should aim at making decisions and take the "right action," which achieves "the best" for the team and the project, representing a rather normative and positivist approach to the ethics concept.

Jepsen and Eskerod (2013) discuss ethical issues toward project stakeholders, briefly addressing "professional, social or moral standards" as the basis for identifying ethical behavior without further elaboration on the theories.

This section focuses on ethics in academic sources, but many of those sources draw from the publications of professional bodies. It is worth mentioning that project management professional bodies have developed codes of ethics and professional conduct, providing general guidelines and articulating some of the values regarding ethics in project management (Loo, 2002). Though these have been helpful for establishing a common language to be used in project management practices (if they do), there is a common consent among many academic scholars that the field needs a more fundamental approach to developing an appropriate body of knowledge on ethics in projects if project management hopes to address the real ethical dilemmas in modern project organizations (see, for example, Bredillet, 2014; Helgado'ttir, 2008; Loo, 2002; Müller et al., 2013; Walker & Lloyd-Walker, 2014). It is also disputed whether "self-regulating approaches" to ethics through a cultural aware-ness are more likely to succeed than "directly" introducing codes of ethics for practice (Brien, 1998, cited in Müller et al., 2013).

Ethics or codes of professional conduct do not appear as a chapter, a topic on their own, or even in the indexes of project management publications produced by Frame (2002), Gardiner (2005), Lock (2013), Turner et al. (2010), and Pinto (2013), to name a few. However, frequent references to at least the instances of ethical issues in project failures have inevitably been made.

Classifications of the Ethics Theories in Project Management Literature

Different classifications of ethics theories are addressed in related project management literature. Helgado´ttir (2008) refers to "out-come-oriented" versus "process-oriented" ethical theories. In the former (Helgado´ttir, 2008), "the outcome or the goal of one's ac-tions dictate its integrity or rightfulness" (p. 745). Outcome-oriented theories could either be *virtue ethics*, with a focus on one's (the proj-ect manager's, in this context) satisfaction with his or her own con-duct, or *utilitarianism*, in which one endeavors to keep others happy as far as possible. On the other hand, process-oriented theories in-dicate that the processes leading to the outcomes define whether an action is right or of integrity. These are broken down into *deonto-logical ethics* and *natural rights theory/social contract*. The former dictates: "Act only according to that maxim whereby you can at the same time will that it should become a universal law" (Kant & Wolff, 1969, cited in Helgado´ttir, 2008, p. 745). The latter emphasizes acts that consider other people's rights and respect.

Loo (2002) uses five normative ethical theories as the basis of his study of ethical dilemmas in project management. These are justice, relativism, egoism, utilitarianism, and deontology, fol-lowing from Reidenbach and Robin (1990, cited in Loo, 2002). Central ideas of each theory are defined as follows: *Justice* refers to the distribution of good and bad; *Relativism*, to culture-based definitions of ethics rather than a universally accepted norm;

Egoism, to individuals' concerns for the implications of their actions in the long run; *Utilitarianism*, to creating the highest level of benefits against damage; and *Deontology*, to individuals' duty toward others based on an ethical rule.

Another approach classifies ethical theories and discussions as "normative," "descriptive," or "behavioral" (see, for example, Jonasson & Ingason, 2013). Jonasson and Ingason (2013) discuss *normative* versus *descriptive* approaches, in which the former provides "guiding principles and tools," while the latter describes "ethical situations, norms and behaviour" without offering guidelines (pp. 16–17). Mishra, Dangayach, and Mittal (2011) associate descriptive ethics with decision making in business and management and suggest that such theories attempt to "predict" people's ethical behavior in certain situations besides simply explaining what they actually do.

Addressing the multidisciplinary nature of ethics studies, Müller et al. (2013) refer to the approaches of philosophy, theology, and the related disciplines as *normative* and those taken by psychologists and other social scientists as *behavioral*. According to the authors, normative ethics deals with what people "should" do in certain circumstances and on what basis (principles and norms) (Müller et al., 2013). Based on their emphasis, such theories are categorized as *deontological ethics* (process oriented), *consequentialism* (outcome oriented), and *virtue ethics* (character oriented) (Müller et al., 2013). Bredillet (2014) refers to *deontological ethics* and *consequentialism* as classical normative theories, which have traditionally been the bases of the development of the existing codes of ethics and professional conduct in project management.

Ethical Dilemmas and Ethical Decision Making in Project Management Literature

Clear definitions of ethical situations and ethical dilemmas are not given in the related publications in project management, despite frequent reference to the terms and the fact that there is no common consent on what each might encompass. According to Walker and Lloyd-Walker (2014), situations involving a choice between two "equally undesirable alternatives" (p. 568), which necessitate making an ethical decision can be referred to as "ethical dilemmas."

Jonasson and Ingason (2013) argue a slightly different viewpoint on dilemmas while criticizing the use of "absolute terms" of a "single right and wrong" in the ethics context. They define dilemmas by saying: "The very fact that it is a dilemma means that this single truth may not be the same for all stakeholder groups" (Jonasson & Ingason, 2013, p. 11). Hence, they emphasize the necessity clearly communicating decisions and the logic behind them.

Jepsen and Eskerod (2013) also address the difference between stakeholder views, associating ethical dilemmas with situations in which there is conflict between the "professional, social or moral" (p. 71) standards and the behavior that seems to be best for the project. In a study conducted by the authors (Jepsen & Eskerod, 2009) on the practicality of the current approach to stakeholder analysis, they only find one instance of ethical dilemmas addressed by the participants.

Moral and ethical decisions or dilemmas can be distinguished from other types of decisions as a result of their source. In such dilemmas, the decision might lead to "material and psychological consequences" to others while violating the rights and creating "conflicts between opposing claims" (Garcia & Ostrosky-Solis, 2006, cited in Mishra, Dangayach, & Mittal, 2011, p. 341). Another view the authors refer to associates such decisions with some of the individuals' "core values" besides containing "uncertainty and possibly unknown consequences" (Guy, 1990, cited in Mishra, Dangayach, & Mittal, 2011, p. 341). Jonasson and Ingason (2013) also highlight "ethical decision making" as the fundamental rather than peripheral component of project management; hence, they replaced "better ethical decision making" with "better decision making" (pp. 16–17).

Generally, ethical dilemmas can have either internal or external sources (Kerzner, 2013); can occur throughout a project, regardless of its life cycle phase; and can happen for any of the parties involved in the project (Walker & Lloyd-Walker, 2014). It is also observed that people react variously to each individual ethical challenge they might face and that different people may react differently to the same dilemma, even in the same organization dealing with the same ethical challenge (Walker & Lloyd-Walker, 2014).

Some authors, such as Gray and Larson (2011), Kerzner (2013), Müller et al. (2013), Müller et al. (2014), and Walker and Lloyd-Walker (2014), have provided examples of ethical issues and ethical dilemmas. Only the last three sources provide a classification of dilemmas. Gray and Larson (2011) define dilemmas simply as situations in which it is difficult to decide whether an act is right or wrong. They provide examples of such situations, referring to a study that revealed 81% of project managers had faced ethical dilemmas; however, they do not provide the study's details (Gray & Larson, 2011). Kerzner (2013) also provides plenty of very tangible instances, classified as internally versus externally driven, though he does not refer to a systematic study as the source of the lists.

The works of Müller and his colleagues (Müller et al., 2013; Müller et al., 2014) are based on two systematic studies aimed at exploring the relations between ethics, governance, and trust. They provide clear lists of three primary and four secondary categories of ethical issues extracted from their research besides the four dilemmas clearly formulated. In their paper, they map these against four different governance structures (Müller et al., 2014). Walker and Lloyd-Walker (2014) focus on the client side. Their study is based on an in-depth single case study, addressing a clear set of issues and dilemmas.

Toward "Behavioral" or "Descriptive" Theories of Ethics in Project Management

Reviewing the most recent project management literature on ethics reveals a common consent on the insufficiency of normative ethics theories in a project management context (e.g., Bredillet,

2014; Bredillet, Tywoniak, & Dwivedula, 2015; Brien, 1998, cited in Müller et al., 2013; Jonasson & Ingason, 2013; Müller et al., 2013). However, one can hardly find agreement on what type of theories should replace these. Claiming that normative theories dominate the project management literature, Müller et al. (2013) suggest that the field would benefit from more research on, and links with, behavioral ethics in order to provide more fundamental insights into "why" people basically "engage in unethical conduct" (Müller et al., 2013, p. 30).

Bredillet (2014) proposes a new "Aristotelian" perspective to ethics in project management to replace the existing normative codes of conduct developed by professional bodies. This view implies a transformation from the question "What is my duty?" to more fundamental questions of "why" and "how"—"Why should I undertake my duty?" and "How ought I act in this situation?" (Bredillet, 2014, p. 559) The transformation intends to overcome the deficiencies of normative approaches, as "ethics cannot be reduced to a system of rules, although some rules are uninfringeable. Ethical theory illuminates the nature of virtue but what a virtuous agent must do in a particular situation depends on the circumstances" (Bredillet et al., 2015, p. 11).

Two examples in the reviewed literature focusing on the necessity of ethics education for project managers have some behavioral elements—the studies by Loo (2002) and Helgadóttir (2008). Interestingly, neither work has been tested with undergraduate or postgraduate student participants. Hence, despite the value of the outcomes and the efforts they discuss, the impacts of participants' lack of acquaintance with the complexities and multiple dimensions of the ethical issues in real projects need to be considered.

The explorations of Müller et al. (2013), Müller (2014), and Walker and Lloyd-Walker (2014) involved real project management practitioners; hence, they provide more realistic perspectives on behavior in ethical studies. All three studies address areas for future research.

According to Müller (2014), behavioral studies of ethics in project management investigating "why people or organizations behave (un-)ethically in projects" from social science and psychological perspectives are scarce. To promote awareness, there is a need to provide more appreciation of the causes of unethical behavior and to conduct more behavioral studies.

Concluding Remarks

This chapter has provided an overview of the current status of ethics studies in project management, drawing from some of the key publications in the area. This overview has included the definitions of ethics in project management, categorization of ethical theories used within the project management context, and examples of ethical dilemmas. Finally, it addressed the inclination of more recent studies to distance themselves from normative theories through conducting more behavioral studies. There is a need to rethink ethics in project management with the aim of embedding it in the different aspects of the field, both in theory and practice.

Our current study of responsible leadership in projects is placed in line with contemporary trends, most specifically because of its descriptive rather than normative approach. It is also distinct from other studies in terms of using longitudinal data, so it has the ability to reflect the dynamic and changing nature of ethical issues and dilemmas.

CHAPTER 5

Ethical Decision Making

Introduction

There has been considerable focus on unethical behavior and decision making in recent years, as concerns regarding their impact and consequences have been laid bare through successive corporate scandals and questionable business practices (Muolo & Padilla, 2010). Within the academic community, this has spurned interest in how individuals arrive at ethical decisions. An ethical decision is a decision "that is both legally and morally acceptable to the larger community" (Jones, 1991, p. 367). The first review of studies in the area of ethical decision making was published just over two decades ago when Ford and Richardson (1994) summarized much of what was known to that point about factors influencing how people make ethical decisions. Since then, three further reviews have appeared in the literature, reflecting increasing interest by researchers in seeking to gain a better understanding not just of factors that influence whether ethical decisions are made, but also how ethical decisions are made—i.e., the ethical decision-making process itself (Craft, 2013; Loe, Ferrell, & Mansfield, 2000; O'Fallon & Butterfield, 2005).

Individual and Situational Factors That Affect Ethical Decision Making

Much of the early work in the field has focused on identifying individual factors that shape how people see or interpret ethical or moral dilemmas. Chief among these have been gender, age, education, employment background, nationality, religion, personality, and personal values (e.g., Brady & Wheeler, 1996; Kohut & Corriher, 1994; Singhapakdi & Vitell, 1990). Interest in these latter two variables, in particular, has gained increasing momentum, possibly because they lend themselves more easily to practical applications for organizations, such as the recruitment and selection of employees, but also because they reflect the Aristotelian notion that what can be judged as ethical behavior is that which illustrates values such as trustworthiness, honesty, and integrity. Craft (2013) highlighted 43 key findings in the area of personality in her review. This included studies examining how the Big 5, locus of control, mindfulness, self-control, and Machiavellianism influenced whether individuals acted ethically. Much of this research suggests that personality factors can influence how people see ethical issues and how they then respond. Ruedy and Schweitzer (2010), for example, found that individuals with high awareness of their own thoughts and their external environment, referred to as mindfulness, considered it more important to uphold a higher moral standard. Similarly, individuals with a higher internal locus of control were more likely to take responsibility for acting ethically (Forte, 2004). Watson, Berkley, and Papamarcos (2009), on the other hand, showed that individuals who placed great value on power and were more hedonistic were more likely to act unethically when the rewards were significant.

How an individual's personal values influence ethical decision making has also attracted significant attention. Values such as egoism, idealism, justice, utilitarianism, relativism, and deontology are among those more widely studied because they serve as the basis upon which ethical judgments are made (Douglas,

Davidson, & Schwartz, 2001; Groves, Vance, & Paik, 2007). So, whereas idealists believe that ethical principles always hold true regardless of the context, relativists see ethical standards as much more dependent upon the nature of the situation as well as on cultural and societal factors. Individuals who subscribe to more utilitarian beliefs tend to judge an action as ethical dependent upon the outcome, often framed as the greater good. By contrast, those with a more deontological perspective dismiss the focus on outcomes as an appropriate means for making ethical decisions and instead place greater emphasis on the role of universal laws that should guide how decisions are made (Amirshahi, Shirazi, & Ghavami, 2014).

Researchers have long recognized that individual factors offer only partial insights for explaining ethical decision making. Instead, an interactionist perspective highlights the importance of situational factors as well. A number of variables have been studied that fall into this category, including peers, organizational culture, ethical culture, codes of conduct, as well as societal norms. In the latter case, differences in societal norms have been found to influence ethical decisions (Sims & Gegez, 2004). An ethical culture comprising ethical standards, practices, incentives, leadership, and personal relationships has been shown to positively impact ethical decision making (Elango, Paul, Kundu, & Paudel, 2010; Shafer & Simmons, 2011; Sweeney et al., 2010). Similarly, organizational culture has been found to be associated with ethical awareness and the decisions made (Ho, 2010; Sweeney et al., 2010). The impact of peers and management as a situational factor has been a further contextual factor that has received considerable attention (Flynn & Wiltermuth, 2010; O'Fallon & Butterfield, 2005). Peers and social groupings have been shown to play a significant role in individuals' beliefs that their decisions or actions would be considered ethical by others. The importance of social consensus and its role in ethical decision making has consequently been highlighted as a significant factor in a number of ethical decision-making models that have appeared in the literature.

Ethical Decision-Making Models

Much of the research in the area of ethical decision making has tended to focus on the individual and situational factors that can influence how individuals perceive ethical dilemmas and issues. Much less research has focused on theory development (O'Fallon & Butterfield, 2005). Nevertheless, several models have appeared in the literature (Hunt & Vitell, 1986; Jones, 1991; McDevitt, Giapponi, & Tromley, 2007; Rest, 1986). Perhaps the most popular models are those developed by Rest (1986) and Jones (1991). All of these models tend to present ethical decision making as a purely cognitive process that is framed through predominantly rational concerns (Park & Stole, 2005).

Rest (1986) posited a simple, four-step model of ethical decision making and behavior that characterizes the ethical decision-making process as proceeding sequentially through the following stages: (1) moral awareness: involves the individual recognizing the issue as having moral concerns; (2) moral judgment: involves the individual deciding which set of responses is morally correct; (3) moral intent: involves the individual resolving to place moral concerns above others; and (4) moral behavior: involves the individual acting on the moral concerns through moral intent. Jones (1991) subsequently built on Rest's (1986) model to develop his model of moral intensity. This is defined as "the extent of issue-related moral imperative in a situation" (Jones, 1991, p. 372). The model depicts the outcome of the ethical decision-making process as dependent upon the extent of moral intensity perceived by an individual. This comprises six dimensions: (1) magnitude of consequences—the perception of harm or good that may arise as a result of the decision taken to people involved; (2) social consensus—the extent to which an individual believes others would act similarly in the same circumstances; (3) probability of effect—the individual's appraisal of how likely it is that the perceived outcomes of the decision will actually occur; (4) temporal immediacy—the amount of time the individual believes will pass between the present and the perceived outcomes; (5) proximity—the extent to which the individual is close to those involved; and (6) concentration of effect—the perceived strength of the consequences for all those affected by the individual's decision.

Despite the popularity of these two models in influencing much of the research to date on the ethical decision-making process, they have both nonetheless fallen under increasing criticism. Chief among the criticisms are that these models fail to recognize that ethical decision making often occurs under conditions of high uncertainty and equivocality that significantly influence how individuals perceive ethical issues (Sonenshein, 2007). These conditions often lead individuals to reach ethical judgments through intuitive processes, in which emotions play a much larger role (Steenhaut & Van Kenhove, 2006; Vitell, King, & Singh, 2013). This would suggest that the major emphasis placed on moral reasoning in these highly rational, cognitive models is unlikely to capture the way people actually make ethical decisions in real-life organizational settings. Indeed, one of the problems with much of the research offering support for these rationalist cognitive models is that it is mostly informed by experimental studies that focus on a narrow set of variables associated with these models, often using scenarios (Thiel, Bagdasarov, Harkrider, Johnson, & Mumford, 2012). Even within this body of research, only the social consensus and magnitude of consequences factors have received consistent support (O'Fallon & Butterfield, 2005). This conceptualization also runs counter to much of what we know about decision making more widely, where concepts such as bounded rationality (Simon, 1955) have found support in research showing that people rarely participate in the extensive reasoning suggested in these cognitive models (Bargh & Chartrand, 1999). In organizational settings, then, the notion that managers must first recognize a problem as being a moral one, and next apply their moral philosophy to reach an ethical decision, becomes somewhat more tenuous.

With these limitations in mind, there has been some attempt to overcome the lack of theoretical development in this area (O'Fallon & Butterfield, 2005) with alternative conceptualizations of ethical decision making that recognize the process as essentially one highly dependent upon an individual's sensemaking (Sonenshein, 2007; Thiel et al., 2012). In circumstances where people are unable to see the future consequences of their actions, they experience ambiguity regarding the best way to proceed and engage in sensemaking in an attempt to navigate their way forward.

A sensemaking perspective (Weick, 1995) suggests that individuals are likely to construct alternative meanings of the ethical issues they face, influenced by their expectations and the motivations that arise out of their lived experience. This places the aspects of socialization and identity at the center of ethical decision making and shapes the meaning we create about ethical situations. How individuals interpret meaning from such situations thus becomes a key focus for understanding the ethical decision-making process. Sonenshein (2007) has incorporated these ideas into his sensemaking model relating to ethical issues. This recognizes that how people respond to these issues is likely to be influenced by the social stimuli surrounding them at the time. This alternative model comprises three stages, labeled (1) issue construction, (2) intuitive judgment and explanation, and (3) justification. Through issue construction, individual, social, and environmental factors are seen as important in understanding how people give meaning to a situation. Individual factors (including motivations and expectations) shape how people see a situation because individuals are likely to rationalize the meanings they give on the basis that other members of their social group will also perceive as legitimate (Ashforth & Anand, 2003). This, then, means they will test out the legitimacy of their meaning through interacting with key others. Sonenshein (2007) refers to these as social anchors. Other factors, though, can affect this process, such as the pervading institutional logic regarding what is acceptable or expected behavior. This suggests that the more aware an individual is of others' mental models or ways of seeing the world, the more he or she will feel confident in constructing meaning from situations. Whether a situation is recognized as having ethical implications or not thus becomes highly affected by the context.

The second stage in the model, intuitive judgment, places far greater emphasis on individuals' feelings that occur instantaneously once they have constructed meaning from a situation. Affect is seen as the foundation for any moral judgment that is then made, rather than any extensive cognitive processing (Krebs & Denton, 2005; Krebs, Denton, & Wark, 1997). Finally, Sonenshein (2007) suggests that any rationalization that does occur in the decision-making process, occurs afterwards. Here, individuals explain and justify their decision subsequent to meaning making and the use of intuition rather than at the beginning of the process as suggested in rational models. Sonenshein (2007) argues that a chief reason why these sensemaking processes have not been detected in previous research lies with the extensive use of scenarios in ethical decision-making research. These often utilize examples of ethical dilemmas that fail to capture the uncertainty and equivocality more typically found in real-life situations.

Sonenshein's (2007) sensemaking-intuition model is arguably consistent with a number of perspectives and findings from other research. These have sought to place emotion and interpersonal factors more centrally in our understanding of ethical decision making (Detert, Trevino, & Sweitzer, 2008; Gaudine & Thorne, 2001; Henik, 2008; Mumford et al., 2008; Woiceshyn, 2011). Arguably, then, the emergence of sensemaking models represents an advance in the development of a theory to understand ethical decision making. However, empirical work that applies a sensemaking perspective to study ethical decision making has been far more limited to date. We seek to overcome this limitation by showing how aspects of sensemaking can be shown to explain how ethical decisions were addressed in the four projects we studied over the course of a 12-month period.

CHAPTER 6

Research Aims and Methodology

Specific Aims

The aims of the study are to investigate the enablers and constraints to responsible leadership in projects through exploring the ethical issues faced by project managers as they interact with project members and their stakeholders and how ethical decision making occurs in projects.

Research Questions

1. What personal-value conflicts arise for project members on projects and what are the values or mind-sets that direct their decision making?
2. How do interactions with stakeholders reveal insights into ethical decision making on projects?

3. What are the norms that regulate how project members deal with personal conflicts in projects and to what extent do they provide an ethical orientation for project managers?

Research Design and Setting

We employed a phenomenological approach to map the inter-relationships among personal conflicts, ethical issues, decision making, and their impact within four projects within the finance industry in the United Kingdom. Drawing upon a processual, in-depth case study approach (Yin, 2003), we analyzed the series of interpersonal interactions and ethical issues that arose among project managers, their team members, and stakeholders over the course of 12 months in four projects. All of the projects were located in the same organization, which provides an extensive range of commercial products, including homeowners and business insurance, pensions, and investments. As researchers, we were unable to choose specific projects to study and the projects were not chosen randomly. The company did, however, offer us the opportunity to examine two large-scale projects that were focused on transformational change in the organization, and two smaller projects that were focused on product development.

Data Collection

We conducted interviews with the project manager, the project sponsor (a senior manager in the organization), and at least one other member of the project team at three-month intervals over a 12-month period. Specific details of those interviewed and the nature of these projects are provided in our descriptions of each case study. We conducted a total of 60 interviews. This enabled us to capture the ongoing and iterative relationships between ethical issues, decision-making processes, actions, and impacts, and how these changed in response to context and over time (Pettigrew, 1987). Each of the interviews lasted between one and two hours.

The interviews were carried out in the interviewees' workplace in accordance with the guidelines and codes of conduct recommended by both the British and American Psychological Societies (APA, 2002; BPS, 2009). Each member of the research team was allocated one project and undertook all the interviews with the members of that project. We also took field notes during interviews and used these to supplement our transcribed interview data. Repeated interviews with the same individuals gave us insights into how the nature and content of ethical challenges and personal conflicts were changing and how previous actions and decisions gave rise to further personal conflicts or ethical dilemmas.

Data Collection Methods

We developed an initial interview protocol (Appendix) that drew upon theoretical models of ethical decision making and sought to identify situational impacts on ethical decision making (Stenmark & Mumford, 2011). We used the Critical Incident Technique approach (Butterfield, Borgen, Amundson, & Malio, 2005; Edvardsson, & Roos, 2001; Flanagan, 1954) to minimize the risks of generic or socially desirable responses and focused on identifying specific behavioral data before gaining deeper insights into the cognitive and affective circumstances surrounding the incident. We framed this through asking how interviewees' values had influenced their recent decisions, actions, and behaviors, or for examples where value conflicts occurred. We considered this the best approach to access the type of data we were interested in, rather than using a blunt approach that asks interviewees to consider questions of morals or ethics. All interviews were recorded and transcribed to form the core data for the analyses.

Trustworthiness of the Data

We sought to maximize the trustworthiness of our data through: (1) taking written notes during interviews in order for researchers to check back on their understanding of what was said and to clarify any early inferences drawn in interviews; (2) checking data gathered from interviews about decisions and actions taken with information contained in any relevant project documents requested and supplied in order to triangulate findings (Strauss & Corbin, 1998); and (3) having the research team meet four times during the course of data collection to check our inferences with one another and to ensure that there was agreement that the inferences being drawn were reasonable based on the data.

Data Analysis

We utilized an iterative approach to our data analysis that proceeded alongside our data collection. The regular meetings of the research team enabled us to share data and cross-reference our data against the literature. We made use of the constant comparative method (Glaser & Strauss, 1967), where we drew upon previous theory in ethical decision making to identify the nature of particular constructs deemed relevant and how these then interacted within the broader project systemic environment. Each case was initially analyzed to identify four key themes: (1) the range of personal value conflicts experienced in these projects and how they were perceived, (2) the nature of the decision-making processes taking place, (3) how the decision-making process informed subsequent actions taken, and (4) how the context affected decision making. We then undertook more in-depth data analysis in which data sets were coded to identify major themes and categories. After each round of data collection, we analyzed data and met as a team to identify case categories. Data analysis thus consisted of three distinctive stages: (1) coding individual interview transcripts, (2) cross-case comparisons within the same project, and (3) coding across sources (Miles & Huberman, 1994). Our final set of data analyses gave rise to separate sets of coding categories for each project. These are presented in four tables corresponding to each one of the four projects we studied and are located in Chapter 10 of this report. Each case was then written up independently to best illustrate the key findings that emerged in each project.

CHAPTER 7

Findings:
Four Case Studies

The Company in Which the Four Projects Are Based

The organization in which the four projects are based is a major insurance company in the United Kingdom. The company is a mutual and owned by its members (customers). The company offers a wide range of products, including general insurance, life insurance, pension investments, and risk management services. The delivery of the products and services happens through direct sales and a service center, as well as the agency network. The company counts more than 300 offices located in rural towns and villages. Farming accounts for 50% of the customer base. The company had a poor history of success in implementing projects and, particularly, large-scale programs. The executives were concerned that a previous program for the life insurance business had failed to deliver after three years and a cost of £20 million. In general, the company recognized that part of the causes of failure was a general lack of capability in terms of change management.

7.1 Alpha Project

Background to the Case

Alpha Project commenced in October 2014 and is expected to be completed in 2018. It is a continuation of the life services transformation program the company had undertaken two years previously, but it was considered not to have made a significant impact on the life insurance part of the company. The previous project had been a technology-based change program, but it had not achieved the strategic ambition of doubling the size of the life insurance business. The aim of the Alpha Project was to bring the life insurance side of the business into profitability. This would involve a £30 million investment by the company. A strategy document was produced by senior managers that identified this objective. At the start of the data-collection process, the project had just finished the start-up phase, or what was referred to as the "as is." This involved defining what the life business currently looks like, or the scope operating model. The project was beginning to identify where the company wanted the business to be. This focused on transforming the initial strategy paper regarding the life business into operational objectives.

The project was run by external consultants who were selected for their knowledge of the business sector and the particular way in which they work. A key problem identified by the senior management team prior to undertaking this project was that the organization was quite risk adverse. This had led to considerable delays in decision making on projects. The external consultants were considered best placed to lead the project to deal with this issue. There are no project managers or business analysts from the organization on the project. Instead, this is a very small project team that consists of three people from the external consultancy and five team members from within the business. These internal team members only comprise subject matter experts from customer services, sales, IT, and finance. The project team has been located off site, away from the main business headquarters where most members of the staff are based. The project team, referred to as the core design team, report to a steering group that comprised two members of the board. The director of strategy and marketing was a key sponsor of the project in the initiation phase. The sales director was the sponsor for the execution phase.

Those taking part in interviews at different stages of the data-collection process encompassed the external consultant commissioned to lead the project as project manager, a subject matter expert from the area of customer services from the life division (customer services expert), and two key stakeholders who were at different times the project's sponsors: the director of strategy and marketing and the sales director.

The Ethical Dilemma

The aim to increase the profitability of the life division focused on introducing new technology platforms. This would transform the key business proposition—in particular, how life insurance was sold to customers and the nature and range of products offered, with ramifications for how the business should be structured. This meant that staffing would need to be reduced. Over the course of the research, this became a key focus for trying to gain insight into the ethical decision-making process. Specifically, the ethical dilemma centered on to what extent and when staff should be informed that bringing the life insurance side of the business into profitability would result in a number of staff members losing their jobs.

Findings

Recognizing the Moral Issue

From the start of data collection (Time 1), members of the project team and the project's steering group recognized that the business transformation would require efficiencies to be made and that there would inevitably be job losses:

> "So it's really clear this project is about profit, that's what it's for, it needs to make a hole in the £7 million loss, which means

there is a revenue strategy and there is a cost strategy. We have four key initiatives that we are going to do with the revenue, there are some sub-ones, but four key ones, and then with the cost reduction that's going to be people and the small amount of IT cost reduction." (Project Manager)

"Well, there's a very big implication on the life business and people working in it because one of the things that we are doing is we're going to be outsourcing a very large part of our manufacture and that will impact on people's roles and almost certainly will mean a reduction, and it will be significant." (Director of Strategy and Marketing)

All those interviewed justified the need to transform the business and accepted that this will have an effect on staffing based upon a strong belief in customer service and to ensure the sustainability of the life side of the business:

"At the heart of all of this, I've always tried to do what is best for the customer in there and actually that's quite difficult because actually a lot of the people that could potentially be impacted are friends, are colleagues, but I think you have to stick with what would the customer expect and it goes back to how do you make something profitable, how do you make the life business actually succeed and work?" (Customer Services Expert)

"There's the natural tensions in business between looking after staff and customers and the progress of the business; they are ethical challenges, but I think if you keep firmly in the mind that in our company more than any other—I mean, we're owned by our customers, therefore we have a duty to deliver the best service that we can so that is the strongest ethical beacon in my mind—nobody here has a right to be here unless we are delivering what the customer wants . . . while recognizing that there will be pain for some of the staff along the way." (Director of Sales)

The recognition that outsourcing was to play a significant role in the business transformation meant that a chief ethical dilemma was how staffing reductions were to be justified and when it would be appropriate to inform staff what the impact on roles and jobs would be:

"So that was very important so we get alignment, agreement, and joint accountability . . . so I've made it very clear to the team we want to be open with people, show them everything you are doing. There are some things that we are going to get on to which is around cost cutting that we can't be open with everybody, but key people we can do." (Director of Strategy and Marketing)

"Probably the one that's coming to light at the minute is as we start walking through the "to be" process, it's quite evident of the roles that won't be there and . . . it's one of those dilemmas. Do you start telling them now about things that are going to happen or, do you wait and it gets announced in one go? . . . Do you start drip feeding some information through or not? So, I'd say that's probably my dilemma at the minute around things, is that I know things, are coming. Do I let people know about that or not?" (Customer Services Expert)

When asked about when it would be appropriate to inform staff that the expected business transformation would result in redundancies, the need to be specific about who would actually be affected was presented as the rationale regarding when would be an appropriate time:

"Actually, we don't know what the "to be" looks like at the minute, we haven't done that piece of work; that piece of work won't be finished probably until about June/July of this year and after that, and we said it at the kick-off event we will then do the communications to people so you won't be in the dark about it. To an extent, I kind of feel as much in the dark about it as everyone else almost, in there because all we're doing is actually saying how do we want the processes to work. Once we've done that, then we can overlay actually how many people

do you need to do that. It might come out quite a bit different; it might not come out too much different on there." (Customer Services Expert)

It was thus clear at the outset of the project that there would be significant implications for restructuring the life insurance division and the customer services expert was aware that this was the case. The project, though, was described in terms of transforming the business to make it sustainable in the long term. Business transformation was therefore seen as imperative in order for the life insurance division to survive. Prior attempts to transform the division were not seen as unsuccessful and the failure of the previous project to turn the business around despite the huge costs invested meant that those involved in the project spoke of huge expectations that they would deliver the changes needed. The historical context of the project and its goals thus initially shaped the meaning individuals attached to the moral dilemma.

Factors Affecting Sensemaking at the First Stage of Data Collection

Some of the key findings from the study highlighted a range of contextual factors surrounding this project and how it was implemented that shaped the customer service expert's (CSE's) sensemaking process. The moral dilemma that there would be job losses as a result of the project was seen initially as justifiable because the project took on an almost reified aspect by those involved, in the sense that it was "saving" the business. A number of differences in how the project was implemented signaled to the CSE the significance attached to this project in this respect. The selection of team members to join the project was a key factor. Data collected from interviewees in the early stage highlighted the emphasis placed on how members of the project team had been purposefully chosen. In addition to expertise in a functional area, the people selected were deemed to have similar mind-sets in terms of how they might approach working together as well as a commitment to the need for business transformation:

> *But getting the right people on that small team was really important and the right people weren't necessarily the people that were offered up, and I think that was a key piece. So we wanted people who had the right sort of expertise, but also the right sense of motivation. I don't want to say value set because that's wrong, but behaviors would be a good way of describing it . . . so when I think about behaviors, we need people who are focused on doing the right thing for the organization over the long term who are willing to take the lead, be proactive, self-motivated, hopefully positive, willing to just do what needs to get done whatever that is going to take, and who are able to collaborate effectively." (Director of Strategy and Marketing)*

The decision-making process on the project was also changed with a view to increasing accountability and the speed with which decisions were made. Again, this served to emphasize the "imperative" nature of the outcomes of the project to the survival of the life insurance side of the business. Historically, the decision-making process within the organization was viewed as being slow, cumbersome, and lacking accountability:

> *"We like to do things by committee. Now, that has a lot of benefits in that everybody is on board supposedly and all the rest of it; the difficulty with that is you've got possibly 20 people in the room supposedly making a decision—probably not going to happen. So things can take a long time. Accountability can be quite unclear. Who actually is accountable for that decision?" (Director of Strategy and Marketing)*

Behavioral norms were established by the project manager that decisions had to be made within a very short time frame. This helped maintain momentum to keep the project moving through each step. There was a general view that this was a positive aspect of the decision-making process, in that individuals were forced to declare their perspective on a particular issue rather than ignore it or seek to obfuscate:

> *"[We need to] make these decisions and make them now and, in particular, the ones on cost, and we're putting forward some very, very serious things that need to be decided, but if you want your objective, if you want it, then you are going to have to decide that—and now—otherwise there's going to be a problem." (Project Manager)*

This had two major implications. The first was that members of the project were able to develop close working relationships very quickly, resulting in a high level of team cohesion. The second was that this enabled the project team to generate a set of behavioral norms where sharing perspectives on problems was talked about as a critical project success factor, but also where establishing a common and shared position as each step of the project progressed was seen as a critical aspect of how the project functioned. This even extended to how relationships were managed with the steering group. Here, there were high levels of political activity involved in securing agreement to each of the recommendations for business transformation that were put forward by the project at each step and that needed to be signed off by the steering group. This was seen in the way the project manager and other key individuals met with each member of the steering group individually prior to the sign off at any board meeting:

> *I think it all sounds really manipulative, but I think you have to know the people; I think you have to know who those key stakeholders are and you have to really understand what's making them tick . . . what are the things that are going to prevent them from acting or whatever in the way that you would like them to, so it's getting to know them actually, and if I can't build the relationships, can I find somebody who already has a relationship or can build one? So, I think a lot of it is about*

that relationship piece and getting to know people." (Director of Strategy and Marketing)

Again, to facilitate the decision-making process, the project team had occupied an office some distance away from the main building where many of the staff were employed. This was quite different from how projects normally operated in the organization:

"Having a small focus group was very positive, they're all in one place, it's dynamic, they're very clear on what each of those individuals' objectives are, and the decision-making process is much quicker." (Director of Strategy and Marketing)

Early on, then, the project took on an exalted status, which reified the significance attached to it by the organization. This was signaled by bringing in an external consultant to lead the project, not only because of his technical expertise, but also because he was unencumbered by the organizational culture, which was said to be averse to making the hard-headed business decisions that senior management believed were needed in this project. Major emphasis was placed on selecting the right people as subject matter experts to work on the project, and not everyone put forward for the project was selected. Instead, the individuals selected were seen as committed to ensuring the long-term profitability of the life insurance division, in addition to being seen as highly talented with future career potential in the organization.

The external consultant also introduced a new approach to decision making that further signaled the importance attached to achieving the needed business transformation. This was typified by ensuring that all decisions were shared by the project team as well as by the steering group. Accountability for all decisions was dispersed across the project's members and by stakeholders in the steering group. Intensive lobbying by members of the project with steering group members ensured that everyone involved in the project was committed at each stage of the project's progress. At this early stage of the project, then, the context was such that the moral dilemma associated with the CSE constructed the expected impact of business transformation on staff as one associated with the goal of *saving* the life insurance business. The selection process for project members served to reinforce the perception of how important this project was to achieving this goal. It also meant that this perception was shared by all those selected to work on the project. The decision-making processes for how the project would operate and interact with the steering group emphasized urgency and similarly reinforced this perception of the project's importance. The primary people with whom the CSE interacted shared a similar perception regarding the project's importance in achieving the sustainability of this part of the business. The organizational culture was one where customers were placed at the heart of all decision making, and this, too, had a major influence on how the moral dilemma was interpreted. All those interviewed described the importance of transforming the business in terms of being able to offer a far better proposition to their customers. Ensuring the profitability of the life business was therefore perceived at its core as meeting the needs of its customers above all else. Locating the project in a separate building offsite also had the palpable effect of reinforcing the special status of the project and the extent to which senior management placed great store on what it was doing.

Factors Affecting Sensemaking at the Second Stage of Data Collection (Time 2)

At the time when the first visit was made to conduct interviews, the project was in the initial phase where the focus was on documenting, in fine detail, how the life insurance business currently operated. This included a complete audit of all work processes as well as staffing ratios. This initiation phase also involved developing differing scenarios for how the new business would look. By the time of the second visit, much of this work was complete, although the project had taken three months longer to get to this point than had been expected, in particular when it came to consolidating what the operating model would look like with cost and revenue numbers:

> "Okay, so we've done a lot of work around the 'what does the business really look like right now in detail' and I think we've closed all of that off and we're very comfortable and confident we've captured everything at a very detailed level, which is fantastic. We've established what we want the business to look like in the future markets, products, etc., and we're clearer about what that operating model will need to look like and we've started costing that and putting revenue numbers against it, so we're in the middle of developing the business case and we're going to be going to the board in July." (Director of Strategy and Marketing)

At this stage, an outline structure had been developed based upon volumetric data, taking into account the number of insurance cases expected each year, the amount of sales, and partial surrenders. This had been overlaid with the number of staff needed and the roles that would be required. However, there was no decision at this stage to inform staff that redundancies were likely. It was at this stage that the ethical dilemma of when to inform staff of the impact of the business transformation became a more central focus of the case study. The customer service expert was responsible for customer services within the life insurance division, and much of the restructuring and impact on staff would fall within her area. How this project member dealt with this issue provided an opportunity to examine the factors influencing the way the decision-making process unfolded. Some key insights emerged at this stage. First, the importance of sharing decision making within the project team continued to be an important factor in justifying the business changes being proposed and how much information was to be disclosed to the staff:

> "I probably feel like I've got quite a lot of control and I think that's what's quite different this time. So, the way [the project manager] runs it is actually that design team makes the

decisions so we're there to make the decisions, and for those decisions, then to go up to board and to steering then to be ratified and make sure that that's the right way that we want to go with it. . . . We've all fundamentally accepted that's what we want to do and that's what then goes up to the next layer to the likes of the board." (Customer Services Expert)

Second, the detailed plans for how the business was to change had yet to be approved by the board. Stakeholder management was again emphasized to ensure that the decisions made by the project members were likely to be ratified by the board:

"We have a period of four weeks beforehand where obviously that gets walked around with more senior stakeholders just to make sure that, yes, everything is covered; I guess just try and reduce any comeback when it goes to board, just make everything is ticked off and covered." (Customer Services Expert)

The need to keep staff on board and aware of how the project was progressing meant that staff briefings were undertaken as a typical part of the change management process. However, the CSE reported that a recent communication briefing had not gone as well as expected:

"So, we did our own core brief in which [we] said there is nothing to say [about the project] yet . . . It's not going to have seal of approval until July's board. And they're not just going to sit round for two hours and go 'yes, tick the box' . . . it's going to take a few reiterations, so probably don't expect anything probably until about September or October time. . . . It landed very well; there was no comeback or anything, but unfortunately, we had corporate comms then issue the corporate core brief slides and they had put something in the speaker notes at the bottom which contradicted what we'd said. A user [who] sat in services would have looked at it and gone, ah, so you are outsourcing protection now and actually you are in the procurement stage because that's how it read." (Customer Services Expert)

This served as a trigger to raise this project team member's anxiety regarding the salience of the ethical implications of the decisions they were making. They were now particularly conscious of what they said in front of staff and the need to be cautious and deliberate in how they responded to staff inquiries:

"I guess it's embedded in us now; it is a front. You are like two different people with things, but it does make you always stop and think. I was always one of these people. I probably would have just gone in and wanted to try and tell people because I wanted them to be included, whereas now you do have to, you listen to the question and you think actually is there a hidden agenda on that, how am I actually going to approach it, and it's always just that factual, all we can share is the 'as is' stuff." (Customer Services Expert)

The emotional impact appeared to be mitigated to some extent by the physical separation of the project team from the main site where most members of the staff were based:

"In my head, it's because it hasn't been signed off yet, so it hasn't been approved. We haven't got all of the facts yet, but we know the direction of travel that we are going to go into it. As a person, I probably spend more time at [the offsite project team location] now and I guess that you'd probably say that's for a reason of actually I don't have to associate back with people who I've worked with in the past." (Customer Services Expert)

However, despite some practical benefits in terms of having people colocated and sequestered in order to focus attention and improve decision making, the customer services expert on the project indicated early on that this had caused some anxiety among staff as to the aims of the project:

"So, even going over and sitting at [offsite location] away from all the offices, there's nothing secretive about it, there's nothing; it's more just you can put things on the walls, you

don't have to worry about people walking in and seeing things that they shouldn't. Everyone just thinks that's a conspiracy." *(Customer Services Expert)*

The emotional impact of the ethical dilemma on the CSE also needs to be understood within the context of the wider organizational culture. There was a general consensus among those interviewed that the organizational culture was demonstrably caring for its staff:

"The culture is a warm culture, very customer-focused culture, where people have a good sense of why they are here, which is unusual for insurance companies generally, so the staff are wired into a purpose, which is very helpful because it means that if we can articulate change in terms of what we need to do for our customers, that resonates very powerfully back." *(Director of Sales)*

But this culture also meant that staff had a general belief in the long-term security of their employment. It was said that employees often felt they had a job for life, to such an extent that there was said to exist a naivety as to the potential consequences of business transformation projects in terms of their impact on staffing. Indeed, the outcomes of previous projects were criticized for failing to achieve their ambitions for the business through addressing the efficiencies that were thought necessary by senior management:

"We took a slightly different approach with this one, partly because we failed a couple of times in life [insurance] before to get this right; we have a really good clear strategy now and plan of attack. But one of the things that we haven't done well enough in the past in that initiation period is really important—being absolutely clear on your requirements for the future, what your future will be, [what you] future proposition and Target Operating Model is really going to look like, and absolutely in depth, what you have now so you can really, really understand the

capabilities and things you need to put in place. That piece of initiation is something that typically, historically, we haven't done that well, so I agreed with the board that we'd have an extended period of initiation." (Director of Strategy and Marketing)

The culture could be said to be high levels of caring, which meant projects rarely produced impacts that would have significant implications for staffing. This being the case, the organization's culture can also be seen to have influenced the decision to engage an external consultant to take on the project management role and drive the project. Although this was explained in terms of the lack of technical expertise internally in this area, it was also clear that the project team would not be subject to these constraints:

"The other thing is execution in our organization where higher degrees of conflict are required potentially; sometimes it's easier to bring a different style in to the organization that has a slightly more bulldozer effect, if you see what I mean. So, for example, on the Alpha Program, one of the guys who is the consultant has a very abrasive approach to execution and stuff gets done and there is usually a small trail of destruction behind him, which we go and point out that this guy doesn't work for us in the long term; it's a short-term pain, but spit and get on with it. That sense of temporary discomfort for a significant change is more palatable if that person then leaves later. So, you are almost importing something the body would naturally reject within the culture to get something done and then letting it be rejected and depart." (Director of Sales)

Indeed, the external consultant (project manager) reinforced this by commenting:

"So, when somebody says we need to make a profit, I can't even describe how seriously I take that. I mean, like totally and utterly if that's what you want, that's what you will have and we will leave no stone unturned. . . ." (Project Manager)

Despite the anxiety associated with the decision not to inform staff of the likely consequences of the life insurance business restructuring, the CSE seemed to rationalize this to some extent by seeing herself as best placed to secure the best outcomes for staff in her area:

> *"However, I guess I do look forward and think actually how will this land when people do find out, but then still in my head was actually someone has to do this, so I think if I looked at it on the opposite side and say I was one of the people back at the [main site] and there was another person on the project, I'd probably look at it and go, well, I'm glad actually they did have somebody; this wasn't just driven by external consultants just clicking their fingers and going yes, we'll just go with that."* (Customer Services Expert)

By the time of the second visit, the CSE reported some anxiety as a result of a communications briefing to staff that had not gone so well. This centered on some information in a PowerPoint presentation that appeared to suggest outsourcing some of the life insurance division's work that was not supposed to be communicated. This "trigger event" served to raise the implications of the business restructuring for staff so that it became more salient in the CSE's awareness. Her emotional response to the moral dilemma appears to have played a role in how the issue was then reconstructed in order to deal with it. Here, although the importance of customer was still a key factor in how the moral dilemma was perceived, it seemed that the CSE had undertaken additional rationalization for why staff members were still not going to be informed of the impact of the business changes. The first rationalization was that she indicated that major decisions still needed to be signed off by the board. This meant they weren't in a position to say anything to staff because authorization by senior management had yet to be secured. The second rationalization was that although staff redundancies were a reality, she believed they would be in the best position to look after the interests of the staff as a whole. The emotional impact of the moral dilemma continued to build as the project progressed and the impact on people's jobs became clearer.

Factors Affecting Sensemaking at the Third Stage of Data Collection (Time 3)

Three months later, there was still no firm communication to staff regarding the expected impact on staffing as a result of introducing new technology platforms and outsourcing much of the life insurance business. This was continuing to be a source of tension for the CSE:

> *"The comms is a real difficult one to manage and I think that's probably the one that, if I was to say something keeps me awake at night, I'd probably say comms . . . because everyone has their own style of comms. So sales are sat there thinking, do you know what, this is fantastic for us; they haven't got the people implications to it, so why can't we just go and say what we're doing; it's fantastic news, the board have signed it off and this, that, and the other, and of course, we in services, I sat there going, we can't say anything yet. And there's always this conflict a little bit. . . . To me, it's more that these are colleagues, friends, and things like that, and where I would hate to think is that they think, well, she's known about this and I'm part of the project and all."(Customer Services Expert)*

By the third visit, the CSE indicated anxiety, but also a sense of guilt, that she had been keeping information from their colleagues. At the same time, however, the CSE talked about how the organization's caring culture had given rise to widespread complacency that staff members could expect jobs for life. Again, however, it was stated that the organization needed to change and the need to serve the customer was paramount. By the time of the final visit three months later, a number of significant business changes recommended by the project had already been implemented and a number of staff affected by the changes had been informed that their jobs were at risk. The CSE talked about the extent to which the organization had attempted to mitigate the impact of restructuring through attempting to redeploy as many staff members as possible and that various support strategies had been implemented to assist those staff affected.

Factors Affecting Sensemaking at the Final Stage of Data Collection (Time 4)

During the following three months, the project had progressed so that the team had selected a new protection provider, were in the process of selecting a RAP (remote access portal) provider, and were introducing a new customer relationship management tool in the life services division. This stage also saw the beginning of those staff members affected by the restructuring being informed as to whether there would be consequences for their roles and, in some cases, their jobs:

> *"Our team leader population have got very edgy over, well, what does that mean to me, so they can kind of see numbers dropping from below, numbers dropping from above, and they are sat in the middle and without lying to them that, yes, cost is still, we haven't stopped yet, so if we feel we have to do anything more then we will do it." (Customer Services Expert)*

It is important to note that the organization was also going to great lengths to minimize the impact on jobs through redeploying staff elsewhere in the organization, and had been following a process where positions were not replaced through natural turnover:

> *"[We] also treat our people as sensitively as we can and find as many opportunities for them to stay on mission, if you like, finding different ways for them to help clients that is still commercially viable, but reuse people where we can as much as possible and those unfortunately that we may not be able to,*

*we treat them with dignity and respect and say thank you enor-
mously for their work." (Director of Sales)*

It seems apparent from the above that the way the customer
services expert engaged in ethical decision making does not fit
well with a rationalist approach to understanding the ethical decision-making process. The rationalist approach construes the
process as managers first recognizing a situation as being a moral
one, and then applying a set of moral principles and rationalizations to inform a moral judgment regarding the decision. Instead, this case suggests that how the customer services expert
viewed the moral dilemma shifted as time progressed, and her
interpretation of the situation varied as different events unfolded
during the life of the project. Although she initially interpreted
the meaning of the business transformation in heroic terms as
saving the life insurance division, the personal impact on staff
gained increased salience as events and personal interactions
with those staff members affected brought the moral dilemma
into sharper perspective. This, then, increased in its intensity.
This supports the view that the ethical decision-making process
in an organizational context is seemingly more akin to an ongoing negotiation of meaning in response to events as they unfold.

7.2 Beta Project

Background to the Case

This case relates to a program within the property and casualty division of the business. Within this division, the company provides
both domestic and commercial covers. Core to the performance
of property and casualty insurance is the ability to underwrite and
rate risks that are offered for cover, and ensure that a premium
is set that covers the risk and contributes to the profitability of
the business. This is a highly competitive market and price competition is rife (particularly within the area of domestic covers,
where the explosion of comparison websites focuses customers
on price). The long-standing customers have strong relationships

with the agents who represent the company. This results in "special pleading" and "deals" on price across the business.

The executive team recognized that the profitability of the property and casualty business was not good and that this position was not sustainable. The executives also recognized that the company's ability to rate risk was far from adequate and well below the standards of the competition. Within the program, there are four major projects: (1) acquisition and installation of a rating engine, (2) migration of legacy systems to the new rating engine, (3) development and implementation of a Target Operating Model (TOM) that establishes the parameters for all risk rating, and (4) integration with the management information system. The overall program has a planned budget of £30 million and is scheduled to be completed over a five-year period. This case examines the acquisition and implementation of the rating engine and had a target implementation date of August 2017.

The overall program was established with a philosophy of providing "fair and accurate" pricing. This guiding philosophy was a reflection of the need, as a mutual, to be concerned about equity for members as well as profitability of underwriting. This philosophy was to be embedded in all projects within this program. The executive decided to appoint an external contractor to undertake the role of project director. The person appointed was selected because of his successful track record in implementing major changes in other financial sector organizations.

Ethical Dilemma

This project was established to dramatically improve the company's ability to price risks and focused on the development of a new targeting operating model for risk rating. The executive recognized that the new Target Operating Model would have significant implications in terms of restructuring and job losses. This was a cause of concern because the company tended to pride itself on not having to make any staff redundant in the past. Two major ethical challenges/issues emerged. The first of these was the challenge of adhering to the philosophy of "fair and accurate pricing" as positioned by the executive while ensuring that an effective rating system was successfully established. The impact of the external and commercially focused project director, and the subsequent engagement of other external contractors, tended to privilege commercial effectiveness over equity for customers. This dilemma tended to be more acutely perceived by the full-time employees and their interpretation of "fair and accurate pricing" was clearly impacted by the culture of the organization.

The second ethical challenge that arose related to the development and implementation of the Target Operating Model. A significant aspect of the overall program was the development of a new property and casualty operating model that would entail significant restructuring. Although this change was known about from the outset of the project, it only emerged toward the completion of the first stage at the end of the first year of the interviews. However, the project members decided not to make the implications of the new TOM explicit at the start of the program. The ethical dilemma concerned when it would be appropriate to inform staff members affected by the changes that their jobs may be at risk.

Key Informants

The interviewees for this case were the following:

- The Project Sponsor, who was a direct report to the director of property and casualty business and responsible for the operations in this line of business
- The Project Director, who was an external contractor/consultant on a fixed-term contract for the duration of the program; he had been appointed on the basis of his broad experience of leading complex projects in financial services organizations
- The Project Team Member, who was a subject matter expert who had worked within the business in the area of risk rating

Findings

Recognizing the Moral Issue

The core purpose of the program was to deliver "fair and accurate pricing," and this was seen by all interviewees as something that would benefit the organization and its members. Although they all bought into this purpose, there were some differences in its meaning for them. Both the project sponsor and project team member saw this as an ethical purpose in line with the core of the organization. The project director, however, saw it as more of a commercial imperative. These viewpoints tended to inform the various team members' respective approaches and commitment to the project. This core ethical purpose was particularly dominant in the project team member's approach to working on the project and his belief in its value:

> *"What is really easy is the fact that the rationale behind everything we are doing on [the project] and the ethics behind it all means that it's a really good sell even when prices are going up or down. So, fair and accurate prices is a lovely thing to work with. . . . What we are doing with price goes to the very heart of who we are as a mutual." (Project Team Member)*
>
> *"Fair is a really interesting word, kind of Freudian debate, but fair to me in commercial terms, because I am [from] a very commercial background, would be that I don't go out of business actually so if I'm charging my customer too little it might seem that's incredibly fair, but actually from a contractual point of view it's actually unfair because it's in the longer term, it's not sustainable, so fair is very interesting, but the accurate bit of it is undoubted." (Project Director)*

In our last interview, the project team member felt concerned that the ethical purpose of the project had been lost and that the focus was more on the commercial aspects of the pricing strategy.

Consequently, he felt less committed to the project and to a future career with the organization:

> *"It's quite difficult for some people because some people don't necessarily want to see that vision; they want to see detail or they want to know exactly what impact we're having or whether we're to time, time scales, and whether we are actually going to deliver it or whether it's just a young chap talking about ideals." (Project Team Member)*

The way project members perceived restructuring also revealed differences between both the employed members of the team and the consultant/contractor. The project director had been brought in based on his wide experience of implementing large-scale projects in a diverse range of other organizations and he drew on this experience in framing his views on the way in which this project should be handled. The executive, program sponsor, and project director recognized from the outset that this would be a difficult change to implement. It was evident that the restructuring would give rise to significant redundancies—something the organization had not experienced before and that sat badly with the company's paternalistic culture. As a result, consideration of this decision was deferred to a later stage in the program. It was at this point that a notable difference between the views of the external project director and the employed members of the project team became evident. The project sponsor reflected the project director's lack of willingness to address this issue from the outset and the preference to defer difficult decisions:

> *"What we were talking about, it's not just a technical change here; there's a massive cultural change to the way we do things, so actually being able to change in the business successfully, it's going to mean some quite difficult choices we are going to need to make about current teams, I suspect, when we get to that point." (Project Sponsor)*

This understanding of the issue was also clearly understood by the project director:

> *"Around the Target Operating Model and one of the things that might be interesting to think about in future conversations is that at the moment and needs must the Target Operating Model and the program main are two separate things. . . . So, I know this is going to be a real stretch, so yes, one of the most difficult bits of the program is the transition itself, but the impact on the program makes it even worse." (Project Director)*

The project team member was unaware of the implications of the Target Operating Model until toward the end of the interview period. Thus, the dilemma was one primarily faced by those in leadership roles within the project and program.

Handling the Ethical Challenges/Issues

The analyses indicated that the main ways in which the two core ethical challenges were handled were as follows:

Stakeholder Engagement

During the interviews, considerable priority was placed on managing internal stakeholder relations. It appeared that the significance of external stakeholders was perceived as being embedded within the purpose of the project ("fair and accurate pricing"). Throughout the interviews, stakeholder engagement was a dominant theme highlighted by all three interviewees. Given the background of earlier project failures, this was seen as critical to the success of the project by both the sponsor and the project director. Although the focus on stakeholder engagement was seen as one of persuasion and influence by both the project sponsor and project director, the project team member saw engagement more in terms of informing and educating.

The theme of stakeholder engagement remained pervasive throughout the period of the interviews. However, as the project demonstrated successful progress, there was a growth in confidence that eased the challenges of engagement. However, it was interesting to note that, as the project progressed, the engagement of the employed project team member was impaired as he saw a shift from the perceived ethical purpose of the project to a more commercially oriented one:

> *"Just to add fuel to the fire, we've brought a consultant in who, again who is challenging whether we go after fair and accurate prices in the same way as we thought we would at the start of last year. He's thinking that optimization is that profit optimizing." (Project Team Member)*

In general, it was seen that the effort put into engagement led to an improvement in the decision making around the project. All interviewees agreed that decision making within the organization tended to be slow and characterized by constant requests for further details and information. However, there was an agreement that, as a result of the effort put into engagement with stakeholders, the speed of decision making (particularly by the executive) had improved notably:

> *"Making it very clear and giving people the information to make the strategic decisions has meant that people haven't become frustrated; they understand that pitch and they understand why we are making the changes we are and it's worked actually, to this point, really well." (Project Team Member)*
> *"So that kind of confidence thing that we built up and that kind of pre-work that we do as you say talking to people now means that we get decisions, we need more quickly." (Project Director)*

Leadership and Team Development

In dealing with the ethical challenges, both the project sponsor and project leader appeared to place emphasis on their role as leaders in building a strong project leadership team and developing a committed and skilled project team. They worked to engage team members through open and extensive communication both with individuals and with the team as a whole:

> *"So I think the leadership team is absolutely key. Change programs are about people, not about anything else." (Project Director)*
>
> *"I think because we have got very good open communication channels, which is part of the leadership piece, that we're in a good place. We're getting on very well together actually." (Project Director)*

The view of senior leaders tended to be reinforced by the experience of the project team member.

> *"The team's purpose and entity is pretty good, actually. We seem to be knitting together more, which is great. . . . As I said earlier, it's been made easy because we're progressing and the business is more comfortable with Beta and the ship as an entirety, and I think that's down to leadership doing a really good job." (Project Team Member)*

However, when it came to the leadership approach to the implementation of the Target Operating Model, some real differences emerged. The project director tended to be less open in his communication with the team. In part, this was in response to the board's reluctance to broach the issues of restructuring at an early stage:

> *"Because of that structural change and the people that will impact, it has to be handled in a very sensitive way and so that target operated work is [an] operating model where it's been handled outside the main program." (Project Director)*

However, this was a view he did not necessarily agree with:

> *"Having been involved in considerably bigger restructuring pieces, Company A and Company B, where we dealt really directly with the individuals involved and warned them ahead of them being formally at risk that that's where it was headed,*

that's the way to go for me. But that's not the way that they've chosen to do it here." (Project Director)

Indeed, at a later stage in the project, the project director was consciously limiting the openness of his communication with the team:

"I get appraised; I know what's going on, but that's not shared more widely. Nor should it be; it is a balancing act." (Project Director)

During this phase of the study, the project team member's perceptions of the leadership changed and led to a loss of commitment. The lack of transparency in communication, particularly around the process for placing individuals in new roles and selecting those who would be made redundant, was seen to be somewhat unfair to internal staff (some 50% of appointments being external hires):

"In terms of actual handling of the message and the delivery of it and whether it's the right thing to do, I think some of the communication in the department could have been better; . . . I think if we wanted to, we could have reshaped some of the experience in the department; I think there's a huge amount of untapped potential that we're not willing to go and tap into and invest in getting the most out of people. Instead, we just want to make those current skills redundant and go to the market and try get new skills . . . you know what you have to live with, but I think we could have done it in a nicer way." (Project Team Member)

In addition, the levels of involvement were seen to be less authentic and leadership decisions tended to be more designed to force through changes, and input or challenge was no longer welcomed:

"If you start making noise that nobody wants to hear, it's not going to go down well. . . . It's not my job; I need to know my place." (Project Team Member)

Overall, it was interesting to see the impact that the decision—to avoid addressing the issues associated with the implementation of the Target Operating Model openly and at an early stage—impacted adversely on both the commitment of project team members and their perceptions of the leadership team.

Factors Influencing How Project Participants Made Sense of the Ethical Dilemma (Sensemaking)

In exploring the factors that might account for the ways in which participants made sense of the ethical challenges, two interrelated strands were identified: decision-making processes and the organization's culture.

Decision-Making Processes

The need to build confidence in the project and recognition of the risk aversion and requirement for consensus in decision making underpinned the emphasis on stakeholder engagement from the outset of the project. Among the interviewees, there was a strong view that within the company decision making was poor and very slow. This was seen as being notable when engaging in large and complex projects. The approach to decision making was seen as entailing a high need for consensus and a high degree of risk aversion, requiring a high level of detail and reworking of proposals for change or new initiatives:

> *"Steering meetings are for making decisions and what then tends to happen is, as a collective, we don't make decisions and part of some of that kind of behavior. . . . This organization is very poor at making decisions, that's true, and some of the behavior like that feeds into it." (Project Director)*

One of the common aspects of decision making was the executive team's need for an enormous amount of detail and information before coming to a decision. This was seen as a reflection of the overall risk aversion and experiences of the past failures of projects and programs.

"So, it's a lot of data work and analysis to show how price is working throughout the company at the moment put in a way that an exec team would understand and delivered in one-to-one sessions." (Project Team Member)

"So when people aren't immediately seeing lots of quick wins, that's quite a challenge, but the level of detail as an organization that we seem to want to go down to at a senior level can slow down decision making." (Project Sponsor)

It was apparent that the slow decision making and need for more and more data reduced noticeably when there was evidence that the project was progressing successfully. At a later stage in the study, it was evident that the project was achieving its target deliverables and the experiences of decision making became more positive:

"A pat on the back from the chair saying the program seems to be very well managed and is going very well. So that kind of confidence thing that we built up and that kind of pre-work that we do, as you say talking to people, now means that we get decisions." (Project Director)

Organizational Culture

The aspects of decision making highlighted above reflect, in part, the culture of the organization. Interviewees saw the organizational culture as somewhat paternalistic, risk averse, cautious, conservative, and consensus seeking. As a result, it was perceived to be somewhat slow to change. The company was perceived to be relatively successful in terms of its ability to serve the needs of its members (as a mutual). However, this was seen as leading to a culture that was "sleepy and complacent." This, combined with the company's risk aversion, led to the focus on detail in relation to decision making that contributed to the organization being slow to change:

"A naive person would say lackluster, lacks drive, lacks focus, lacks ambition, lacks motivation, stagnating. I think the more rounded person would say it's a sleeping giant, this place;

there's been lots of passion, there is lots of passion in all these people; it just seems to have been slightly eroded over time and needs—it almost needs an injection of cocaine to wake it up." (Project Team Member)

This complacency and reluctance to change was combined with a strong paternalism and that needed to change:

". . . the organization is 'too nice' . . . it needs to wake up and sharpen up. If it does that, it has a lot of potential." (Project Director)

However, there was also a reluctance to hear "bad news" and to have practice or policies challenged. This, again, tended to lead to a reluctance to change and move forward speedily:

"I think we do have a very static culture of not liking change challenge. We don't move in any direction, we don't change tack." (Project Team Member)

"So, I think there is a reticence in the organization to hear bad news alongside a willingness to go looking for it. I can't explain it any better than that; it's very strange." (Project Director)

The impact of the organization's culture on the project and related changes was a dominant theme throughout the interviews. Within the case, the interviewees saw the culture of the organization as being "traditional," cautious, risk averse, and consensus seeking. This was seen to lead to slow decision making and a strong detail orientation. The culture was also perceived as being somewhat paternalistic and one that emphasized care and concern for employees. The nature of the organization (a mutual) resulted in a core value related to a purpose of "serving our members." This clearly framed the issue construction of the internal members of the project team. The culture was perceived to be accompanied by an aversion to challenge, which was noted by the project team member when he tried to raise issues or concerns about aspects of the project. The experiences he reported indicated that the culture was also hierarchical. Overall, the hierarchical nature of the culture and its resistance to challenge seemed to result in an absence of overt discussion of ethical issues. Furthermore, the issues associated with the restructuring related to the project caused problems when the decisions were finally announced. The focus on "looking after our people" and the lack of experience in handling redundancies resulted in postponing communicating the decisions, even though the need for this change was known to senior leadership from the outset of the project. The delay resulted in a questioning of the ethical behavior of the leadership and, in order to avoid "giving bad news," there was a lack of engagement with the employee stakeholder group.

The slow decision making was also a reflection of a general climate of avoiding conflict and building consensus around all decisions and actions. However, although the culture was characterized by paternalism and consensus seeking, the interviews with the project team member indicated that it was also a quite hierarchical culture. As a result, those at lower levels in the organization felt that their voice did not count and that "speaking up" could be damaging in terms of their career:

> *"If it's someone's idea, we'll just run with it if it's coming from the right person. The idea that someone like me would be taken seriously in a junior management environment because I'm willing to be passionate and actually call things out, no, absolutely it's not; we don't have that sort of culture." (Project Team Member)*

In general, it appeared that those in the team who came from outside of the organization were less impacted by the constraints of the existing culture. This became very notable in relation to the way in which the core purpose of the program was implemented. The project director saw "fair and accurate pricing" as more of a commercial imperative to be profitable. However, the reactions of those from within the company to this development were characterized by a feeling that the organization's core values had been compromised.

The culture of the organization had a particularly strong impact on the second main ethical challenge—the implementation of the Target Operating Model. It was at the stage of implementation that it became apparent that the risk-averse culture, combined with the paternalism, had delayed addressing a key issue. The history of few redundancies and a perception of being a "caring" organization resulted in a great deal of shock and disruption when the process of implementing the TOM began. Many were shocked. However, the external project director saw this reaction as typifying an aspect of the culture that was holding the organization back from growth and development:

> *"Possibly because it just never has before. So, we'll all be looked after, we'll all be found homes, and this new thing, it will just be a new structure that if we need to get some retraining and whatever, it will just happen." (Project Director)*
>
> *"It was very shocking for the teams involved and to me, as an outsider who has been through a lot of this stuff, and I'm not being cynical, not really, but there was a bit of being a bit astounded that people just didn't see this coming more because a big program like this one, trying to put new tools in . . . you wouldn't have to put many two and twos together to work out that, well, something has got to change here and there's probably going to be an impact, but quite senior people were visibly shocked." (Project Director)*

The somewhat "harder" views of the project director were perceived by team members as being reflected in a leadership style that espoused involvement and consultation, but was, in practice, somewhat more directive and went against some core elements of the organization's culture. Overall, the analysis of the interviews has shown a good deal of alignment among all levels within the project in relation to the majority of the themes identified. However, there was a clear difference between the leadership and team members arising as the project moved to the conclusion of the first phase. This seems very much connected with differences in the way senior executives and project members made sense of the core purpose of the project. What remains to be seen is whether or not the apparent damage done to the commitment of team members by the way in which the restructuring has been handled and the behaviors seen to be unethical will impact adversely on the implementation of the second phase of the project.

7.3 Gamma Project

Background to the Case

This case refers to a project tasked with developing an overall IT-based, counter-fraud solution for the company. The project commenced in summer 2014, and the case study relates to what took place during the initiation phase of the project. The aim of the project was to modernize the company's counter-fraud intelligence system" to cover the insurance business, particularly in relation to the activities of three departments or business areas. The three business areas, referred to as BAX, BAY, and BAZ, are the end users of the system. The first phase of the project involved preparation of the project proposal based upon business requirements, and, at the same time, developing the "Request for Information," which sets out the criteria that potential suppliers need to meet. At the beginning of data collection, 13 suppliers had responded to the Request for Iinformation sent out by the project. The second phase of the project was referred to as the Proof of Concept stage, where four suppliers had been selected from those that submitted responses to show how they could meet the business requirements of the three business areas as end users of the counter-fraud system. Following this, the four potential suppliers were refined to a final shortlist of two, who each submitted comprehensive proposals for developing and implementing a new system. During the final stage of data collection of the study, the project was involved in selecting the final supplier and planning to commence the implementation phase.

Throughout the data-collection period, there were ongoing challenges, issues, and disruptions that affected the project. Most of these originated as a result of disagreements among the three business end users and conflict between the project management team and the organization's change management team, who were also involved in planning for this business change.

The Ethical Dilemma

The ethical dilemma in this project concerned the use of some confidential data from one of the largest stakeholder groups in the future system. The source of the dilemma was the company's lack of permission from the data owners and its legal obligations in preserving the initial relevant agreements on such data against value of the data for enhancing one of the business area's critical functionalities. This was a dilemma that continued throughout the study period and caused significant conflict among project team members and on the project board.

Key Informants

- **Project Sponsor:** Besides playing the role of project sponsor, this person was also the sponsor of another organization-wide change project that was running in parallel. His main role in the organization is as chief manager of one of the key departments that is a main user of the proposed counter-fraud system (BAX). The project sponsor also chaired the project board.
- **Project Manager:** The project manager only works on this project. He has been with the company for a long time in different roles, and for the past couple of years, has been managing single projects rather than programs with dependencies (such as the current project).
- **Project Analyst:** He is an analyst working with the project team in the capacity of Business Lead (BL) for BAX representing this business area in the project.

Findings

Recognizing the Moral Issue

The key issue highlighted in this case focuses on the ownership and use of data that were deemed important by the project sponsor and organizational change manager for determining the requirements of a new counter-fraud system that met the needs of the whole business. The particular data in question were "owned" by one of the end users of the new counter-fraud system, who resisted attempts by project members to obtain the data. This end user was one of the key business departments within the organization represented by the departmental business lead on the project. The case highlights the contextual factors that affected how this "ethical issue" was perceived by those involved, and how the issue was handled. The key contextual factors identified as salient were (1) conflicting expectations and priorities by each of the three end users of the counter-fraud system, and (2) conflicting role requirements and identities of the project sponsor, project analyst, and organizational change manager.

Conflicting End-User Requirements and Needs

The final deliverable of the project needed to fulfill the functional requirements of the three main business areas, each of which had differing expectations, capabilities, and strengths. A key source of the conflict that arose on the project originated because each of the end users was examining fraud at differing points in time—that is, at the quoting or issuing stage, dealing with internal or supplier fraud, or at the claim point. Conflicts among the three business area leads over the scope and type of data required resulted in ongoing debates as to which system was going to fulfill its specific requirement. These conflicts became particularly acute once the project reached the Proof of Concept stage. Consequently, managing differing expectations and demands meant the project had major political undercurrents, with power games and struggles often being played out:

> "There was a bit more tension at the business-lead level. . . .
> And there was a degree of potential conflict between how we

describe the requirement of the different areas, and what we would allow to be in scope, in terms of possible sources of data and information." (Project Sponsor)

"We have a number of risks that we are looking at in terms of the scope of the project because of the three business areas, they are very keen on different—I hate the term—different flavors of the system, and are passionate about different areas and bringing a group together to understand the idea that, as a project, we are looking at it as a group with their own interest areas coming in as opposed to this is what you are going to get and the project will deliver everything you want . . . that little bit of tension has taken quite a lot of political maneuvering and management." (Project Manager)

Throughout the interviews, various or conflicting priorities were constantly among the main causes that led interviewees and other stakeholders of the project to be exposed to difficult situations or choices. Resolving these conflicting demands by end users was made difficult because of the role requirements of key individuals involved in the project.

Conflicting Roles of Key Project Team Members

One of the emerged themes in the interviews was the interviewees' occasional explicit or implicit references to some of the conflicting aspects of their own roles or others' multiple roles. These particularly were relevant to the project sponsor, project analyst, and the organizational change manager. The project sponsor was also the business lead for one of the end user departments that were involved in the project. This posed a potential problem for him in attempting to ensure that the views and needs of the other two business departments were heard:

"I'm sponsoring the project, not just from the perspective of my day job as chief claims manager, but also in relation to the needs of the underwriting and financial crime department. . . . So again, from a sponsorship point of view, what I'm trying

to balance is, not glossing over those potential differences of opinion about what we should do, not failing to give each department the opportunity to say why they would like to keep something in scope or to keep a certain supplier still included in the mix, but always to hold the options up against the original core purpose of the project and the original scope that was signed off. . . . So it's fair, it's impartial." (Project Sponsor)

Further complicating the role of the project sponsor was the fact that this individual was also the sponsor of a wider organizational change program into which this project fed into:

"I think the dilemma from the sponsor's point of view that I've got, and which we will have to address at some point within the project, is how do we align the priority of our project with some of the other things that are going on within the group? So, as well as being the sponsor for potentially implementing a new counter-fraud systems project, I'm also the sponsor of another project which is looking at when and how, and, indeed, whether we should change our core [system or not]." (Project Sponsor)

These multiple roles often meant that the project sponsor was aware of particular information from the wider organizational change project regarding changing business strategy or operations that he was not able to make the project team aware of, despite there being significant implications for the project:

"More recently, one of the other things that has been quite destabilizing for the project team, which they wouldn't have known about at the time but I was aware of from a sponsor point of view because I had knowledge of this in my core business role, was . . . we announced some pretty substantial changes to our business structure and our operating approach both within our regional [BAX] team and within our head office [BAY], and that obviously had quite an impact in terms of some of the core project team members, so the senior business lead for [BAY] is going through a reselection process for changing that business

area and then obviously a concern about, well, the shape of the business into which we will be introducing this counter-fraud system when we've got it is very different, so does that change what we're looking for?" (Project Sponsor)

There were similar conflicting role priorities expressed by the project analyst. He had originally worked as a system analyst with one of the end user departments (BAX) and was now also business lead for this department. He thus occupied both roles in the project team. He recognized the importance of supporting the project team, but had a much stronger emotional attachment to his own business department and their priorities:

"The only dilemmas I get are because I'm coming from a BAX perspective, but then I've got the overall project perspective . . . the only dilemmas I have are, is this in the best interests of my area [BAX] or is this in the best interests of the project? Sometimes it's understanding and getting clarity on that." (Project Analyst)

The organizational change manager's role in the project as well as his broader role leading a wide organizational transformational change project was also a key influence on how issues were perceived by project team members. These two roles were believed by the project manager to be conflicting roles with differing interests. Consequently, there was considerable conflict between both the project manager and the organizational change manager. During the course of the research, it also emerged that differences in the "personalities" and "work styles" of these individuals contributed to problems in their relationship. The initial clashes centered on disagreements about the change manager's suggestions that aspects of how the project worked should be changed despite causing slippage in hitting deadlines, while the project manager was determined to keep to the plans as they were:

"That process has gone through with all the proper signatories and signoff that side, but as the new business change manager

came in, it was flagged up that a piece of work that she'd worked on in a [BAX] role wasn't included in the data coming in . . . very quickly that became a big issue that . . . you must put it in, it's got to go in, you've got to have it, we've got to have it in the solution. . . . Now my concern at that point is we're doing well on the project, we're on track, we've got good, we've got our deliverables signed off, and we have focus and direction. All that's blown up again in the last few days . . . and that is a dilemma at the moment. I say dilemma, I say this and it's like dilemma." (Project Manager)

The situation was worsened by the project manager's perception that the change management agenda was being pushed behind the scenes and attempting to undermine his position:

"Now I feel like that person is working with lots of other people around to get his way and I'm finding out, fortunately, the team I have are worried and concerned, so they will inform me so I know what's going on, it's sometimes not helpful because paranoia kicks in. . . ." (Project Manager)

It is interesting to note the project analyst's view on changes affecting the project at the same time and his sense that he needed to act as a broker between the organizational change manager and project manager. Although he never directly named the change manager or talked about their relations, he frequently expressed his concerns regarding how project change requests were dealt with and their impact on time scales and costs of the project:

"I work as a go-between [for] the project manager who is trying to deliver the project on time and successfully and everything like that, and then you've got the business area who may want to increase scope or change the scope. . . . The project manager wants to make sure all those changes are well considered because change can cause problems, can cost money, can delay things, so I find myself quite a lot fitting in this gap. . . .

So, I am in the middle quite a lot looking at all these things that are raised by the business area and then trying to ratify them . . . working between those two different drives. . . . I think we're going to have to probably end up fighting that drive of let's just get it delivered, let's get it delivered because from my viewpoint, I don't want anything delivered that's not fit for purpose." (Project Analyst)

The relationship between the change manager and project manager was also an area of concern for the project sponsor, who, toward the end of the project initiation stage, had decided to take a more proactive role in shaping the relations:

"There is still some ongoing relationship work for me to keep an eye on and that's between . . . as project manager and . . . as business change manager. I think they are working more effectively together now than they were when we spoke last year, but it's still not a perfect working relationship yet. They are very different characters; they work in very different ways and they rub each other up the wrong way a little bit sometimes and one of the things I've decided to do as we get closer to the business implementation end of the project is to have [Change Manager] more directly taking instruction and guidance from me as project sponsor whereas previously she was doing it from a BAX senior business user." (Project Sponsor)

The change manager's interventions were also a sense of friction with the project analyst, who suggested that there was some overlap in their roles that was leading to some problems:

"With the business change manager, there's a bit of a crossover in responsibilities in so much as the business change manager is responsible for business change being introduced to the business and my role is looking after a certain part of the business, so there is certain crossover, so I've had to assist in putting some focus into that area to making sure the business change stuff is fit for purpose for my business area and probably just

making sure that I'm comfortable with the recommendations that are coming from that area I suppose." (Project Analyst)

How the Ethical Dilemma Was Resolved

The approach to resolving contentious issues and arriving at decisions was, in most instances, described by interviewees as based on open discussion and transparency with a genuine motivation to reach some degree of consensus. Decision making was therefore said to be based upon judging the appropriate way forward against some agreed-upon set of criteria. These were centered on the agreed-upon aims of the project and the criteria that had been developed based on the needs of the end users. However, the project sponsor had a clear view that he was ultimately responsible for "agreeing" with any decisions reached. In this respect, he "persuaded" the end user of the system to share the data that they had initially considered unethical or sensitive:

"Involvement in the sense that, ultimately, I saw that as my responsibility to help the project team find the answer. So, how I did it was to facilitate an open debate and discussion, with my role not being the one who over-engineered, over-influences, or engineers the decision, but does put some structure around the decision making. So, it not just being an exchange of opinions, and who shouts loudest gets the answer, but to hear everybody's opinions, and then let's test this back against the success criteria we've chosen for the project. . . . So I would have been prepared to make a casting vote decision as sponsor if we hadn't reached consensus, but my preference is to hold a pros and cons and keep all the arguments up in the air discussion to move logically to a conclusion. But if that hadn't been possible, I would have used a casting vote to decide, or said, well, I don't feel comfortable doing that, it goes beyond my authority as sponsor, to I want to escalate it to one of the other governance structures within the group, but that hasn't been necessary." (Project Sponsor)

"Again, its part of my role; it's not for the project team to worry about that [referring to the dilemma of changes going on outside the project]; what I want them to do is present to the project board and me, as sponsor, the right answer for the business objectives . . . If they then need to be compromised because of some broader strategic prioritization, then they've given me the best information possible to know about the consequences of doing that, but it's at my level and the exec that that choice will be made, I don't expect the project team to have some schizophrenia over whether to do that or not, so I want them to give me the best recommendation and then I'll work out whether it's the right one, taking into account other priorities." (Project Sponsor)

Here, he indicated that relied upon their own network of colleagues outside the project itself, with which to check out their own thinking and arrive at decisions:

"I mean, that just comes from the nature of what a sponsor's role is, from my level of comfort at operating at that level in terms of the types of decisions that might be involved, and I've got a reasonably good network within the business, so if there's an issue that's bothering me about this, I've got folk I can go and talk to, to help work out what the right way of approaching it might be." (Project Sponsor)

It is important to emphasize that, for the project sponsor, referring decisions to the project board remained the way in which decision outcomes could be reached. It was noted that almost invariably the interviewees' strength and sources of confidence in prioritizing and making such difficult choices between conflicting interests and obligations depended on the level of support and confidence they received or expected to receive from their immediate higher-level management:

"So, I can see some kind of contention potentially arriving there and [it] could be quite a serious disagreement . . . if there is a

problem or an issue, the right thing to do is to escalate it, even if it's difficult, because it helps me think through what the right way of resolving it is and if it means someone at that level gets a chance to think through the problem before it really materializes, we're likely to work our way through the problem much easier in the long run rather than saying nothing and hope it isn't an issue and then all of a sudden it's a big issue that everyone has got to solve at short notice and they've had no time to think about it, no time to attune themselves to what the issue might be. So, in my mind, it would be mad not to escalate stuff." (Project Sponsor)

Both the project manager and project analyst tended to perceive their roles in the decision-making process as a "provider of information" rather than being responsible for decision making per se. This, they tended to see as ultimately within the remit of the project sponsor or project board. The project manager saw his role in decision making as primarily concerned with managing conflict among project team members, particularly the end users, so that consensus and agreement could be reached on a way forward at critical decision points:

"A lot of people may have let that go; I was looking at the longer-term view and the impact of it, so I wanted to make sure that we considered it properly and fairly and to see if there was a problem, so I drew together the key people to talk and make sure that they had the same feeling that we needed to address it . . . then, between us, came to the decision that there wasn't a problem, documented it, and then circulated that with the people involved, the two people involved, and the project sponsor to make sure that they were comfortable with the outcome." (Project Manager)

"One of the challenges that a project like this has is that we've been going for quite a long while because we've been doing careful, disciplined work and by one of the risks it's almost a certainty that the world changes around you while you are doing your work. . . . The project manager has done a pretty good job of doing that because he's worked out who he needs to talk to very quickly and then gone off and done that. . . .

His skill set is to think ahead and then take action rather than always waiting for permission first." (Project Sponsor)

There were many clear instances of open, transparent, and participatory decision making involving key project stakeholders. Later, it seemed that these were mainly the cases when he was dealing with day-to-day and non-key decisions. The approach seemed to change the more a decision might be thought of as involving sensitive data or with far greater longer-term impact on the business. In these instances, the project sponsor was more inclined to take decisions himself on the basis of lobbying other senior personnel in the company, and with far more limited and selective involvement of relevant internal project team members. These changes of approach, because of the nature of the problem or task at hand, became particular apparent when critical issues, such as major company changes and the issue of data privacy, affected the project. It would seem to be the case that this networking approach to decision making was very much influenced by the culture of the organization for dealing with "ambiguous" issues and decisions.

7.4 Delta Project—The Agency Telephony Project

Background to the Case

This project is concerned with the restructuring of the telephony service underpinning sales to the customer. The delivery of company products and services happens through direct sales, a service center, as well as an agency network. The agency network includes more than 300 offices located in rural towns and villages and involving more than 2,600 people. At present, about 110 locations use a telephony service provided by the head office, between 120 and 130 locations have their own arrangement with an external company, while a further telephone company serves about 20 locations in Northern Ireland. The remaining locations have arrangements with individual, separate suppliers. The project will create a unique agency telephony system with one external partner that will implement and monitor the system for the whole network. Procedures like call recording and customer compliance (e.g., when taking credit cards over the phone, having the ability to perform in a compliant manner) need to conform to one overall, shared organizational standard. It would also offer the ability to route inbound traffic according to needs (e.g., if a call comes in to an agent, it can be routed to another agent, another region, or to a national service center). This is seen as a major asset against complaints and breaches, with a clear advantage for the company in financial terms through improving the quality of service. It was also recognized that the company's ability to prevent frauds or mismanagement of cases was not adequate for both the business and customer service.

The first step is to identify and select a supplier, a partner that will provide a common system and meet the company's need for a shared, standardized set of operating procedures. After a partner is identified and the contract signed, the next stage of the project will involve setting up a pilot system across 11 sites to test functionality.

The Ethical Dilemma

The ethical dilemma in this instance centered on the decision surrounding the selection of an appropriate partner to supply a new telephony service to the organization that would enable a better-quality sales service to be offered to customers. The project was under pressure to meet time and cost requirements. However, this could mean selecting a supplier that potentially might not be the best one for the long-term viability of the business. This posed an ethical dilemma for those involved in the project. The case describes the decision that was made and factors that influenced the decision-making process.

Key Informants

The interviewees for this business case were the chief information officer of the company, who played the role of strategic project sponsor. His first commitment was to properly resource the team in terms of human and financial capital. This was done through setting the agenda for the project (e.g., creating a common vision and understanding, and selecting practices and procedures to reach the goals, including a consistent time frame and acceptable standards for decision making); creating alignment around the scope and the standard operating procedures; and finally, maintaining alignment on the scope. In the words of corporate governance, "the buck stops with him." This means the strategic project sponsor is responsible for taking the project scope to the board and recommending it for approval. A second interviewee was the technical project analyst, responsible for the rollout of the service and the operations involved. Finally, the third interviewee was the project manager.

Findings

Recognizing the Moral Issue

The ethical dilemma facing the project concerned the selection of suppliers and was found to be uppermost in all the interviewees' minds during the first set of interviews. This was not resolved at this time and became more pressing as the project unfolded over the coming months. A common theme to emerge was meeting deadlines, with some very obvious ethical implications. The project commenced with two candidate suppliers, as it was thought that this would be sufficient. However, there were initial concerns that the costs submitted by these potential suppliers were much higher than expected. There were also concerns about whether these suppliers would be able to meet all the quality criteria contained in the project brief. At that point, the team had to make a difficult choice that would also hinder the potential for delivering the project within the expected time period. This raised an ethical issue about the trade-off between time, quality, and business sustainability associated with the choice of a particular supplier. At this time, there was no consensus on how best to proceed:

> "Lots of people had different views; even the technical guys couldn't decide which they thought was the best, so that was quite a big dilemma at the time as to how we are going to

resolve the many different ways you could connect this equipment in, what is the most efficient, the most cost-effective, the most feasible, the most acceptable, the most future-proofed way of doing it, and that took quite a long time to resolve and to get everybody to concentrate and agree on the right way forward." (Project Manager)

The issue was complicated by the fact that one of the suppliers of the new telephony service had a long working relationship with the one of the key agents responsible for selling the organization's products and services:

"If you can imagine four potential telephony partners we're working with, one has had a long history with the agents themselves and they feel very close to, so one of the issues is are they too close, do they know them too well? So there's a sort of intimacy there, which is useful during operation, but in terms of the supplier selection, sometimes that doesn't help. So one of the issues is, who are we going to choose and are we going to choose our favorite, which may not be the right answer for the business?" (Project Sponsor)

"So there's one particular guy who has been working with these guys for a long time, maybe five, six years, and knows them very well. His view is they are the best, why are you bothering with all this selection process, you are wasting time, these would be a good choice. And of course, we've got a conflict with other people saying, yes, but you are too close to them; you can't see the perspective; we don't think they are the best service; in fact, here's one I like." (Project Manager)

However, it seemed that the project sponsor had already decided that the bidding process for supplying the new telephony system should be opened up to include other potential suppliers:

"So, in the first two seconds you've made your choice up, you've made your mind up, and the rest of the time you spend is just reinforcing your original choice. . . . I think we've probably made

our choice, but we're spending all our time justifying why that choice was right, which is fine, but it does require you to listen to your instincts and say we've made a choice because I have seen projects in this place where you think it's obvious what your choice is, but you just keep going saying I haven't made a choice yet because the process said you would do so." (Project Sponsor)

The project sponsor's aim, therefore, seemed to be convincing the key stakeholders involved in the project of the legitimacy of this decision despite the problems of failing to meet project deliverables on time and because of the additional budget overrun:

"So we're not working with all of them [the agents], but they have an interesting structure . . . we've kept them onside and talked to them about tactics and negotiation and who we are going to work with. So, we've done a fair bit of stakeholder engagement and mostly on an informal basis, so not through meetings; this would be phone calls, dinners, chats, if you like, unscheduled contact. . . . They've appointed a subgroup of people to represent their interests, but we've spent a fair bit of time making sure they are onside." (Project Sponsor)

This need to gain support for this decision from key stakeholders involved in the project was also echoed by the project analyst:

"The interesting bit is the fact that we're running it from head office, but we have, as part of our project team, members of the agency network, which we've never done before. . . . In the past, we've tended to go out, do our thing, and then tell the agents here is our choice. . . . So I felt in order to get full support when we make a choice and when we deploy it, it would be much more useful to have the agents standing by my side when I say we've made a choice and, by the way, these guys, they were part of it. So it's mostly to help us choose the right partner, but primarily to help the adoption when we have made a choice that we get the agents arguing alongside me to say this is a good choice, it's a good deal, and we should adopt it." (Project Analyst)

What became clear during the course of the study was the emphasis the project sponsor placed on "consensus building" as a means to secure the decision outcome. But in reality, that seemed to be more about persuading stakeholders, especially the network agents, to eventually support a decision that, for all intents and purposes, had already been made by the project sponsor. He described the intense level of engagement they had with agents as part of securing this outcome. It was then the responsibility of the project analyst and project manager to work with the network agents to support this decision:

> *"Most of the time, what we've tried to do is involve everybody in our decision-making process and then usually bring people together around the table to discuss pros and cons of what we are going to do and then get a consensus decision, usually a consensus decision and get that minuted, and agreed, and moving forward." (Project Analyst)*

> *"You could say that, as the project manager, I don't take the decision, I just make the recommendation and they have to make the decision, is one cop-out, but in reality, it tends to be you make that decision and get their buy-in to it rather than the other way around." (Project Manager)*

Consensus building was, therefore, the key strategy used by the project sponsor and project team members in order to influence how the key stakeholders involved in the project made sense of the dilemma they faced. Importantly, the dilemma was managed in such a way as to influence the outcome that was reached—that is, what was considered the best outcome by the project sponsor. There was some indication that this was justified on the basis that the network agents might not be fully aware or equipped to realize the scale of the dilemma and its consequences:

> *"So making sure that the suppliers understand the scope of what we're delivering so that helps to drive price down somewhat, and then, on the counter to that, making sure that agents recognize that it's got to be compliant, resilient, and of appropriate*

scale, that we have to get those assurances from the suppliers to make sure they are running in multiple data centers, that they've got all the appropriate accreditation and certification for their management, and compliance, and all the various data regulations that we have to comply to." (Project Analyst)

"So, we've got quite an unusual team there because we have some people from our group program office, we have some people from IT, so we have salaried people and we have some of our colleagues from the agency network who are not our employees; they are our partners, so they own their own businesses. So, we've got some people on the team who are used to dealing at large-corporate level; I mean, we would be in the FTSE 250 if we were quoted, and we've got some people from the agency network who run businesses who turn over £150,000." (Project Sponsor)

There was evidence that the project analyst was drawing upon rational arguments in order to influence the stakeholders to agree to invite more potential suppliers to bid for the telephony system. There were a number of rational arguments put forward by the project sponsors to justify this decision, drawing upon the wider business case to support the costs associated with late delivery. A plurality of stakeholders meant accommodating different needs, but the project team needs to ensure that the network agents understand the price points and commensurate solutions that do not overload the system with features. The agents tend to have small offices and might not understand the needs of a system that deals with multi-thousand users. The main difficulty is to negotiate among different priorities. Although the company wants to steer the right strategic solution, the agents want to be able to negotiate the right solution for them. In the sponsor's mind, you need to know what is most important, but the whole team has to be engaged with the consequences of any decision. One of the key aspects of the decision-making process was the need to share accountability for the decision and to get maximum ownership for the decision to reopen the bidding process to additional suppliers. This meant going back to the company saying the team would not meet the initial deadline in terms of selecting the supplier. On the other hand, this delay of six months meant they would have found the right solution for the company:

"Yes, we have to realize that whatever we chose now is likely to be a platform for at least the next three years and also is likely to set some of our future direction as to how we are going to merge some of the telephony requirements of all our agents with what we do within (the company) business, so we knew that would be setting out our road map and direction for the future, so it was important that we, well, it is important that we home in on the right solution." (Project Analyst)

Yet this also needs to be seen within a broader organizational cultural context where typically decision-making processes were said to be slow and cumbersome, with actual decision making often put off or delayed because of a risk-averse organizational culture. In this sense, it could be argued that securing consensus among the key stakeholders involved on the project offered some degree of "political cover" for the project sponsor and key project team members:

"What I don't want is to make a decision and then throughout the rollout have some of my key decision makers in that process constantly saying yes, but it's not the one I would have chosen, because that just undermines everything, so I'll be very careful to get everybody in the room at that final point and look them all in the eye and get their assurance that they will back the decision even if it isn't the decision that they would have made because that's always the case, isn't it? In the selection process, you rarely get a selection where everybody is unanimous." (Project Analyst)

As for the overall decision-making process, the sponsor was clearly in charge. As sponsor, he had a critical role in driving the decisions and securing signoff by the project board. However, at least on the face of it, this was to be done in a way that demonstrated transparency, integrity, and inclusivity:

> *"We're all going to be open about where we're up to; there isn't any behind-the-scenes dealing or any dark rooms when you say to someone, hey, you do this, then you'll get this deal." (Project Sponsor)*

Yet there was the reality that, despite this, there would always be limits to how far this potentially can go:

> *"Sometimes you can't act on it and you have to just say, you know, I've listened to your opinions or we've taken that into consideration, but we're not going to do that and here are the reasons. But in those cases, I would still like to explain why we're not doing it and just say we're going to have to move on." (Project Analyst)*

Finally, the role of the project manager on this particular project seemed to suggest he was far less involved in the decision-making process. They suggested that decisions on how to resolve important issues on how the project progressed were the responsibility of senior managers in the organization and other stakeholders. Their role seemed to be more about merely implementing the decisions once they had been agreed upon:

> *"Yes, certainly, within this organization, the project manager role is really about getting whatever it is the business wants transferred into something that can be done and then managing that process through—hopefully delivering whatever it was they wanted in the first place, which often changes along the way." (Project Manager)*

CHAPTER 8

Discussion

In this section, we present some of the key insights gained from the study and how they offer us new knowledge pertaining to the research questions we set out to explore. In all cases, we found that interviewees experienced some challenge in expressing the impact of their personal values and emotions in informing what they did and their decision making. This might be because of the technical nature of the project, the technical background of the participants, their personal attributes, and even their gender, or a combination of these factors to different extents. There were many "gray areas" in all the cases presented, making it difficult (if reasonable at all) to judge unequivocally whether a decision or judgment was made ethically, or, indeed, whether the way the stakeholders were dealt with and engaged (e.g., some lobbying and pre-discussions) or disengaged (in the case of withholding confidential data, for example) was ethical or not. Nevertheless, our case study data offer some insights into ethical decision-making processes specifically within project contexts as we saw them.

1. What personal value conflicts arise for project members on projects and what are the values or mind-sets that direct their decision making?

Our findings showed that ethical or moral dilemmas typified by personal conflicts appeared to arise in all four of the projects we studied. This is despite the fact that all four projects ostensibly addressed very different aspects of business transformation. Observations from the cases demonstrate that there are potentially many reasons for ethical issues and dilemmas in project environments, as suggested by Gray and Larson (2011), Kerzner (2013), Müller et al. (2013), Müller et al. (2014), Walker and Lloyd-Walker (2014), and Jepsen and Eskerod (2013). However, all of these did not necessarily end up being ethical situations or dilemmas, nor did those working in the project environments see and identify them as such.

For both the Alpha and Beta projects, the moral dilemma arose as a result of the anticipated consequences of organizational restructuring on staffing and how and when this should be communicated to staff. In the Gamma project, the personal conflicts that gave rise to an ethical dilemma arose because of the lack of clarity regarding the roles, responsibilities, and values of the change manager and project manager. This led to conflict over whether the project should be allowed to overrun as a result of not having received information that the change manager considered key to the project's success and the use of data that had not been authorized by the originators. The Gamma case highlights how project managers' values regarding delivering the project on time and on budget can dominate their ability to see other factors that might need to be considered in the wider, long-term interest of the organization. In the final case, the Delta project highlights how the decision to select a supplier again involved considering weighing the short-term requirements for the project to deliver on time and cost against the longer-term goals of the business.

In all four cases, the need for consensus was the dominant value that appeared to direct decision making. This was influenced by the wider organizational culture, which was said to be risk averse and paternalistic. Yet, this need for consensus appears to have served a wider objective of ensuring that accountability for reaching ethical decisions was more widely shared. The need for consensus to drive decision making, however, shows how the process of arriving at ethical decisions involves a dynamic interplay of individuals negotiating the conflicting demands of achieving project goals within the context of their own personal values, whether those values were about the longer-term sustainability of the company, the needs of customers, or the treatment of staff within the organization. Seeking consensus can be seen as a chief sensemaking mechanism through which the process of ethical decision making unfolded on these projects (Maitlis & Christianson, 2014; Sandberg & Tsoukas, 2015). Sensemaking occurs through social, cognitive, and discursive processes through which individuals simultaneously interpret and construct meaning in order to reduce equivocality. It is described as "a process, prompted by violated expectations, that involves attending to and bracketing cues in the environment, creating intersubjective meaning through cycles of interpretation and action, and thereby enacting a more ordered environment from which further cues can be drawn" (Maitlis & Christianson, 2014, p. 67). The process, therefore, draws upon past assumptions of how things are in making sense of emergent cues from the environment in order to plan future organizing. It is the past-present-future combination that characterizes the complexity of the sensemaking process, shifting between interpretation of events and enactment. The decisions that project members faced that could be characterized as having high moral intensity were subject to negotiations with wide-ranging stakeholders over fairly long periods of time. This often meant that members of these four projects brought their own personal values in interpreting an ethical situation, but also considered the ethical dilemma within a broader context of organizational values and the needs of other stakeholders. Although greater accountability for decisions was identified by those taking part in the study as driving the need for consensus, it also appears that project members made sense of how their personal values influenced their actions through the lens of other contextual factors. So, for example, personal values that extolled the importance of customers at the heart of the business were used to justify how decisions were made. These values were given new meaning through negotiations with others as being about longer-term business sustainability that often incorporated a much harder, profit-driven edge in a number of instances highlighted in these cases.

This "consensus building" was influenced by a number of important contextual factors that included the previous history of the organization. This history was communicated through stories that previous projects had not been successful in delivering real business change. The project members interviewed often explained how they perceived the goals of their project through the need to deliver tangible business results, in contrast to the experience of previous projects. These stories provided a further means through which project members made sense of the personal value conflicts they were facing, and how they sought to resolve or justify their actions. Ethical dilemmas were thus interpreted through the prism of key aspects of the organization's culture—in particular, the belief that the organization had historically not taken sufficient account of the commercial pressures facing the business. This was reinforced by the perception that the paternalistic organizational culture, although thought of as caring on the one hand, was also an impediment to transformational change. In two of the cases, Alpha and Beta, both of which would impact on organizational restructuring, this was further reinforced by the organization employing external consultants as project managers who brought a sharper commercial focus to the projects. This meant the consensus-building process took on a different dimension in which persuasion, politicking, and intensive stakeholder management were major characteristics. This had a significant effect on the sensemaking process in both cases. Here, the ethical dilemma regarding staff restructuring that was poignant for some project members was given meaning in terms of the longer-term sustainability of the business.

It also meant that decisions such as when to inform staff were not easily arrived at and were often protracted.

2. How do interactions with stakeholders reveal insights into ethical decision making on projects?

This need for consensus building was the driver for the high levels of stakeholder engagement and management that we found in all four cases. In both the Alpha and Beta projects, stakeholder engagement was seen as a means to ensure quicker decision making and greater accountability, and as a way to avoid conflict. But stakeholder engagement was also the means through which a common understanding on the goals and outcomes of these projects could be agreed upon and shared mental models established. These shared mental models meant that ethical dilemmas tended to be interpreted within similar sets of principles. Weick (1995) points out that individuals' mental models or cognitive schemas act as filters in shaping what information is attended to in the environment and how it is then interpreted. Individuals can also give meaning to others through categorizing and relabeling situations to generate consensus in meaning that serves as a more concrete basis for action (Smircich & Morgan, 1982).

In the case of the Alpha project, it was when the project member began to come into greater contact with staff members who would potentially be affected by the project's outcomes that alternative and, to some extent, more emotional perspectives became more salient. An important insight here was that, although it was recognized that the business transformation in life services would impact the staff significantly, the question of when it would be appropriate to inform staff members (or withhold information from them) was never articulated by those interviewed as an ethical concern. However, as the project progressed and the impact on specific staff and the numbers became clearer, the need to withhold information from customer service staff was increasingly presented as a value dilemma by the customer services expert (CSE) involved in the project. In that sense, the moral intensity associated with this ethical situation appeared to increase as time progressed and as differing factors became more salient for the CSE. Jones (1991) identifies moral intensity, or the extent of moral imperative involved in a situation, as influencing moral awareness and the subsequent moral judgments that are made. What the findings from this case reveal is how the context in which this moral dilemma occurred appears to have played a large part in how the nature of this moral intensity changed and how the CSE made sense of this moral dilemma over the 12 months during which we collected data.

Sonenshein (2007) refers to social anchors as key members of individuals' social groups with whom they will test out the meaning they have subscribed to a moral dilemma in order to seek legitimacy. Early in the project's lifetime, these social anchors helped reinforce the meaning that the moral issue was about saving the life insurance side of the business to ensure its sustainability. However, other social anchors for the CSE included the staff and colleagues she works with and whom they manage. These are also powerful agents through which legitimacy is tested. As specific events brought more contact with staff as the project progressed, this legitimizing process gave rise to conflicting interpretations of the moral dilemma and alternative interpretations of its meaning (Weick, 1995). These conflicting comparisons would seem to give rise to cognitive dissonance (Festinger, 1957) and there follows a series of post-rationalizations or justifications in an attempt to minimize this dissonance. Although there was a clear dominant rationalization as to the effects of the project on staff restructuring at the beginning of the project, the rationalization process was not static; it changed or was added to in a dynamic way in response to events where certain social anchors became more salient for the CSE. The rationalizations associated with the moral dilemma are, therefore, by no means simply constructed a priori. Rather, they are seemingly altered and may shift according to an individual's interactions with the wider social environment and, in particular, the people in it.

The initial meaning given to the business transformation was influenced by the different ways in which the project operated. This helped support the CSE's sensemaking process, specifically that the moral dilemma needed to be understood in terms of business sustainability. This was reinforced by new decision-making routines that required individuals to share their views and seek joint accountability, thus giving extra clarity to the mental models that people held. However, new meanings arose over time, and the case highlights the prominent role of emotions in influencing this shifting meaning-making process (Gaudine & Thorne, 2001). Anxiety was prominent, and also gave way to feelings of guilt. What was interesting was how the rationalizations then shifted following guilt toward what might be thought of as stern justifications that staff members should not expect a job for life. By the time significant business changes were being implemented and staff members were beginning to be informed of the impact on their jobs, the caring values of the organization were again seen to play a role in how the CSE interpreted the meaning of the moral dilemma.

In the Beta case, we see that the project had been informed by the organization's experiences of past change failures. Consequently, the organization adopted an approach that emphasizes high levels of engagement with internal stakeholders. This approach appears to have led to the successful implementation of the first phase of the project. Furthermore, it may be inferred that, because the organization is a mutual, it exists to serve the interests of its members (customers). Thus, there is evidence in the case that the project was largely perceived to be serving an ethical purpose. However, when viewing the data within the sensemaking framework of Sonenshein's (2007) ethical decision-making model, it is evident that the issue construction of the project director (an external contractor/consultant) and both the project sponsor and team member (employees) differed as the project progressed. These differences were most marked when comparing the experiences of the project director and the project team member. The project team member saw a shift in the focus of the project from "fair and accurate pricing" to a more commercial and profit-focused one. This presented him with an ethical dilemma. However, he felt unable to raise or address this dilemma as a result of his bad experiences with raising concerns at earlier stages in the project. His inability to either accept or address this perceived ethical issue appeared to have an adverse effect on his commitment to both the change and the organization in general. It is possible that, if such a change had been experienced by other employees, the reduction in commitment could have an adverse impact on the future success of the change. These differences in the construction of issues (Sonenshein, 2007) may be seen in terms of contextual factors relating to the organizational culture and related socialization processes, particularly given that the project director was not an employee.

However, stakeholder management was also found to have other effects. For example, the Delta case highlighted the decision-making process associated with selecting suppliers for a new telephony system to the agents responsible for selling insurance products offered by the business. The case highlights how the project manager's wish for the decision reached to be one that was fair, transparent, and ethical involved a complex set of negotiations among project team members, project sponsors, and agents. The nature of the relationships between the project and these stakeholders and how these evolved over the course of the project influenced how decisions were reached at each stage of the project. High-intensity stakeholder management was a key characteristic demonstrated by the project manager. This was seen to play a significant part in enabling the project manager to secure agreement for the project to overrun by six months so that the decision as to which supplier would be selected would be in the best longer-term interests of the company. The decision to do this presented itself as a moral dilemma for the project manager. How stakeholders were subsequently brought into the decision-making process was key to how the project manager was able to resolve this dilemma. What was interesting here was how selling agents as a distinct set of stakeholders outside the organization became as important as the project's internal stakeholders in reaching a decision. The case highlights how decision making became "stretched" over the web of stakeholders associated with the project. The issue of business sustainability, which took account of how best to meet the needs of the selling agents, was therefore championed against the shorter-term goals of the project delivering against time and cost. Here, the organizational culture, with its focus on the customer, was again found to have a significant impact in enabling this to happen. The regular formal and informal meetings with agency partners illustrated the key focus on stakeholder engagement stated to reflect transparency in decision making and gain consensus among those involved. Yet, although this was how it was described at the surface level by those interviewed, at a deeper level it appeared that all parties implicitly accepted that these were strategies to ensure that agency stakeholders "got on board" with the project sponsor's decision. Consensus building, though preferable as a decision-making strategy, clearly has its limits. Elsewhere in the leadership literature, the role of leaders in constructing meaning from often ill-defined events or situations and conveying their interpretation to those around them is widely recognized as a form of sensegiving from which others are able to develop meaning (Foldy, Goldman, & Ospina, 2008). What was also interesting in this case was the importance that the project sponsor placed on checking out his thinking with other colleagues at similar levels within the company. A key feature, then, was the use of networks by these senior leaders where they shared their perceptions and understanding of a situation to generate cross-understanding, which can then create new mental models as other adopt the same beliefs (Huber & Lewis, 2010). This generation of cross-understanding leads to a consensus in beliefs. In doing so, these leadership networks of peers appear to be significant "social anchors" in how the project sponsor generated new meaning.

3. What are the norms that regulate how project members deal with personal conflicts in projects and to what extent do they provide an ethical orientation for project managers?

Findings from our cases highlight a number of factors that appear to influence how norms and values affect how project members deal with personal conflicts (ethical dilemmas) in projects. The most significant of these have already been discussed above, and they arise primarily from the organization's culture. However, the cases also highlight the prominent role of the project manager in establishing norms that have an impact on the ethical decision-making process. This includes establishing the norms that affect how project members work together, engage with stakeholders, and make decisions. The Alpha project demonstrates how the project manager introduced a framework for ensuring that decisions were made quickly within the project team and that everyone agreed to the decision that was made. The project manager was also responsible for establishing a set of norms for how quickly problems the project faced with issues such as resourcing would be resolved by the project's sponsor and steering group.

The Gamma project shows some of the more interesting insights into this area, because this case deals with the conflict that arose between the business change manager and project manager working on the project. In this instance, the change manager was concerned that the decision to select the best supplier for a new counter-fraud intelligence system for the company would be affected by omitting data from an area of the business considered important to inform the final specification. Going back to rework the specification integrating this data would inevitably lead to the project failing to meet its deadline to deliver on time. The project manager was adamant that this should not happen. For him, the need to deliver the project on time and against budget was the most important factor. This, then, led to significant conflict between these two project members, where the project manager decided he had no recourse but to refer the matter up to the project board for the decision to be taken by the board and project sponsor. In this instance, there appeared to be no firm line of authority between the project manager and the change manager, and their areas of responsibility had become blurred. Here, the failure of the project manager to establish clear boundaries of responsibilities from the outset led to ongoing disputes and tensions with the change manager throughout the course of the project. Instead of transparent mechanisms within the project for dealing with conflict, norms became established where dispute issues were ignored and eventually the conflict became more about personalities than about considering the best way to achieve the deliverables expected from the project. For both the project manager and the change manager, the decision of whether to rework the specification became a moral dilemma, but with each person viewing the situation from entirely differing perspectives despite being in the same organization. The dilemma presented two conflicting accounts of which business needs were more paramount: the need for the project to deliver on time and on budget, or the need for the project to ensure that the procurement process for the new intelligence system was based upon the most robust data possible.

Based on our data, behavioral norms are established in these projects that are distinctive of the organization's culture, but are also affected by the particular leadership style of the project manager, and in particular, how the project managers influence the way decisions are made in a project. It is these norms that directly affect how the ethical decision-making process then evolves in a project but without any explicit recognition by project members of whether an issue is necessarily an ethical or moral one. One of the main observations throughout the study was how the differing role requirements of key individuals on these projects clashed with the wider roles and responsibilities they held in the organization. This led to ongoing clashes and conflicts among project team members. Frequently, the interviewees described how they struggled trying to balance their organizational and project priorities and goals. These statements echo the familiar issues of matrix organizations in projects (Pinto, 2013) or the relationship and governance issues described in Müller et al. (2013, 2014). Project team members translate cues from their environment into meaning within the context of the organization's knowledge structures and the previous experience of the individuals involved (Daft & Weick, 1984). However, a key insight we found was how sensemaking is also influenced at the project level by the norms established for how project team members should work together. However, we also found that differing behavioral norms associated with organizational and project roles can complicate the way project team members make sense of a situation and may result in greater ambiguity in the ethical decision-making process.

CHAPTER 9

Summary of Key Findings and Conclusions

Based on the individual case analyses, together with the cross-case analysis, the main findings that emerge from this research study may be summarized as follows:

Although all four projects can be viewed as dealing with issues that have ethical or moral dimensions exemplified by value conflicts, project members tended not to see these issues as ethical ones. Cognitive models of decision making (e.g., Jones, 1991; Rest, 1986) emphasize moral awareness as an essential first key step in the ethical decision-making process. Our findings, however, suggest that in organizational settings, these personal value conflicts are interpreted through the lens of the organization's culture and business priorities so that ethical issues are not explicitly seen as such. This suggests that Sonenshein's (2007) model of ethical decision making, which incorporates a sensemaking perspective (Weick, 1995), offers a more appropriate way of exploring ethical decision making in contexts that are rich in complexity, uncertainty, and ambiguity. Furthermore, we see here examples of how the process of issue construction is influenced through both individual factors and social factors (Ashforth & Anand, 2003). In particular, we see evidence that institutional logic and behavioral expectations and norms also impact issue construction (Sonenshein, 2007) and that these factors are present through the impact of a strong organizational culture.

Our findings suggest that the way project members engage in ethical decision making does not fit well with a rationalist approach to understanding the ethical decision-making process. Rest (1986), for example, posits a four-step model of ethical decision making and behavior that characterizes ethical decision making as proceeding through four stages: (1) moral awareness, (2) moral judgment, (3) moral intent, and (4) moral behavior. Instead, our findings suggest that the way project members viewed a moral dilemma shifted as time progressed and that their interpretations of the situation varied as different events unfolded during the course of a project. Indeed, this may be seen in the context of sensemaking (Weick, 1995): As the project unfolds, project members' understanding of the complex and ambiguous issues becomes clearer and new sense is made during the course of the project. Furthermore, the engagement in ethical decision making evident in this study indicates that ethics tended not to be perceived as normative (Brien, 1998), but rather as behavioral (Jonasson & Ingason, 2013). Indeed, this evidence of the absence of the impact of normative views and the impact of a behavioral perspective supports the arguments and critiques of ethics in project management (e.g., Muller et al., 2013).

Similarly, the moral intensity of an issue or problem was found to vary over time as project members interacted with different people and situations. These served as "trigger" events that resulted in project members interpreting or reinterpreting the moral dilemma in different ways. These were found to provoke cognitive dissonance (Festinger, 1957), which resulted in a series of ongoing rationalizations or a legitimization process to justify the perspective of the situation taken. This, again, suggests that ethical decision making is more akin to a sensemaking process (Weick, 1995) in real-life organizational settings than a sequential, rational, cognitive analysis of a moral dilemma. Once again, further support is provided for the need for an approach that recognizes the dynamics of individual emotions and feelings in the process of decision making (Sonenshein, 2007) and reinforces the limitations of cognitive models when applied to complex and ambiguous organizational settings (Detert et al., 2008; Gaudine & Thorne, 2001; Henik, 2008; Mumford et al., 2008; Woiceshyn, 2011).

Organizational culture was found to play a significant role in this sensemaking process. Indeed, the importance of organizational culture in the context of ethical decision making has been highlighted by a number of researchers (e.g., Ho, 2010; Sweeney et al., 2010). The culture in the case organization was characterized as being paternalistic and caring, although risk averse. A core value of this organization was "serving our members (customers)." Such a core value could be seen as a component of an ethical culture that can have a positive impact on ethical decision making (Elango et al., 2010; Shafer & Simmons, 2011; Sweeney et al., 2010). The culture in this case resulted in decision-making processes being driven by the need for consensus involving a number of stakeholders. Consensus building meant establishing shared mental models that influenced how project members interpreted moral issues in their projects. This finding provides support for the view that a sensemaking model of ethical decision making is impacted by institutional factors that can shape the meanings and sense that people make (Ashforth & Anand, 2003). Indeed, the organizational culture can be seen as providing an important social anchor (Sonenshein, 2007) that underpins sensemaking when people are faced with ethical dilemmas. In addition, it is interesting to note that the projects studied entailed significant organizational changes, and the impact of organizational culture on decisions in the course of change implementation is well established (Burnes, 2004). Furthermore, there is an increasing recognition of the need for significant levels of involvement of stakeholders in ensuring effective change implementation (Higgs & Rowland, 2011).

Consensus building meant that high levels of stakeholder engagement and management were a distinctive aspect of the decision-making process in these projects. This led to greater accountability for decision making and the notion that decision making was shared or dispersed across a wide network of key actors. This played a significant role in shaping how project members interpreted ethical dilemmas and their subsequent actions. Jepsen and Eskerod (2013) highlighted the significance of differing stakeholder perspectives in relation to ethical dilemmas within projects. However, this tended to be seen as a problematic area. From this study, it is evident that high levels of stakeholder engagement and management reduce the levels of conflict with stakeholders in relation to dilemmas and decisions. Once again, there is evidence here that supports the views in the wider change management literature that involving and engaging stakeholders is an important factor in achieving successful change implementation.

History, in terms of the relative success and experience of previous projects in the organization, was a major lens through which project members made sense of and interpreted ethical issues, and in giving meaning to the moral situations that arose on projects. Within a sensemaking frame (Weick, 1995), applied within the context of ethical decision making (Sonenshein, 2007), the history of previous projects is clearly a factor that impacts project members' issue construction process and shapes the meaning that they give to the situations they face. Once again, the context of the projects studied in this research is one of change. Support for the Sonenshein (2007) perspective is found within the change management literature. Higgs and Rowland (2011) demonstrate that an organization's history of previous changes impacts on decisions relating to the approaches to change being adopted and the related behaviors of actors within the change. Ethical situations arose on projects where conflicts were experienced between project and organizational priorities and unclear boundaries of project members' roles and responsibilities. In these circumstances, the project's governance structure was used to help resolve ethical issues that arose. It could be argued that the governance structures provide a means of communicating norms to guide behaviors (Sims & Gegez, 2004) and provide a basis for identifying ethical behavior in the face of ambiguity and uncertainty (Jepsen & Eskerod, 2013). It could also be argued that the governance structure provides a frame for sensemaking in such situations (Weick, 1995). In resorting to governance structures to resolve ethical issues as illustrated in the cases, there was evidence of significant politicking and the selected lobbying of particular stakeholders in order to secure particular decision outcomes. This, again, suggests that ethical decision making was far less of a cognitive, rational process, but instead was subject to actors persuading and cajoling powerful others to secure outcomes that supported their priorities. This provides further support for the view that individual feelings and affect are important elements in any considerations of ethical decision making (Krebs & Denton, 2005; Krebs, Denton, & Wark, 1997).

Ethical decision making is a core aspect of responsible leadership, but the theory suggests that individuals will judge moral situations in terms of absolute moral standards or universal principles (Pless & Maak, 2011). Our findings suggest that ethical decision making in projects and organizations does not mirror this rationalistic perspective. Instead, ethical decision making is a dynamic process where individuals make sense of moral situations through interactions with key stakeholders and engage in a continuous process of interpretation and reinterpretation of the issue as events unfold. This engagement and interaction with stakeholders is a core aspect within the emerging arena of responsible leadership (Doh & Quigley, 2014; Doh & Stumpf, 2005; Waldman & Galvin, 2008). We found that leaders in our study were engaged in sensemaking that seemed to be highly dependent upon contextual factors in the organization, including the organizational culture. It appeared that the leaders' sensemaking underpinned their interactions with project members in the process of sensegiving (Weick, 1995) that, in turn, impacted the sensemaking of the team members.

Overall, our findings show that in a project environment, ethical decision making may be viewed as a combination of normative and behavioral perspectives (Jonasson & Ingason, 2013; Mishra, Dangayach, & Mittal, 2011; Muller et al., 2013). Furthermore, we found that rational models of ethical decision making (Jones, 1991; Rest, 1986) do not provide an adequate basis for understanding the phenomenon in a context of uncertainty, complexity, and ambiguity. This is in line with the broader critiques of such models (e.g., O'Fallon & Butterfield, 2005; Sonenshein, 2007; Thiel et al., 2012). We find that employing a sensemaking perspective (Weick, 1995) provides a more effective lens through which to explore ethical decision making within uncertain and ambiguous contexts. In particular, we find empirical support for the model proposed by Sonenshein (2007) that, by incorporating a sensemaking perspective, provides a useful framework for exploring ethical decision making within a project environment. Within this framework, we found that organizational culture plays an important role in project members' sensemaking in the process of both issue construction and justification.

The literature on responsible leadership is at an emerging stage. However, there appears to be agreement on the importance of ethical decision making and stakeholder engagement to the construct (Waldman, 2011). Within our study, we have found clear evidence that supports these two dimensions of responsible leadership and its relevance to complex and uncertain contexts (Voegtlin, 2015; Voegtlin et al., 2012). In particular, the engagement with a diverse group of stakeholders has been highlighted, and is notable in terms of the data relating to those with leadership roles in our cases. This provides support for the views of Maak and Plass (2006a) and emphasizes the significance, to responsible leadership, of the need for leaders to focus on relationship building rather than power development.

Conclusions

This study set out to offer new and original insights into the nature of personal, value, and ethical dilemmas faced by project managers and the factors that influence how they make ethical or value-related decisions, along with the role that leadership plays in this context. The findings, summarized above, have shown that in the cases explored, the ethical issues and decisions faced within a project management context are influenced by a diverse range of factors. Furthermore, the way in which responsible leadership is exercised plays a significant role in ethical decision making in the complex, uncertain, and ambiguous contexts in which the projects were being implemented. In particular, the significant effort expended in stakeholder engagement and management played an important role in resolving ethical dilemmas and formulating ethical decisions. In this study, we found that the organization's culture had an important impact on framing decision making and resolving ethical dilemmas.

Our study makes a number of contributions to both theory and practice. These may be summarized as follows:

Contributions to Theory

This study makes a contribution to the literatures on both ethical decision making and responsible leadership, as well as to the project management literature.

In many studies of ethical decision making, there is a focus on a normative approach to considerations of ethics rather than exploration as an enacted phenomenon. In the literature on ethical decision making, there appears to be a focus on rational models (e.g., Jones, 1991; Rest, 1986). However, these have been critiqued as they fail to take account of the high levels of uncertainty and ambiguity that are faced in many contexts and the related emotional aspects of decisions. Sonenshein (2007) developed a model that takes account of these additional factors, adopting a sensemaking perspective (Weick, 1995). However, to date there have been relatively few empirical studies that have tested this approach. This study provides empirical data that provide support for the Sonenshein (2007) model and, in particular, show that a sensemaking perspective (Weick, 1995) plays a significant role in the issue construction component of the model.

There is a growing attention to ethics studies in project management literature in recent years (Müller, 2014). However, these studies have tended to be somewhat limited in scope and lack evidence of practice behaviors of project managers (Loo, 2002; Müller, 2014; Walker & Lloyd-Walker, 2014). This study provides insights into the behaviors and actions of both project managers and team members in the course of working on significant projects. Furthermore, the practices, behaviors, and ethical issues are studied here on a longitudinal basis, demonstrating how the impact of a range of factors on ethical issues and decisions played out over the course of the project.

Within the literature on ethical decision making and ethics within projects, there have been assertions that organizational culture is a factor that impacts decisions and behaviors (Ho, 2010; Sweeney et al., 2010). However, there is limited empirical evidence underpinning these assertions. This study provides evidence of the central role that organizational culture plays in the ethical decision-making process and in resolving issues and dilemmas. Responsible leadership remains an emerging concept that suffers from definitional disagreements and a lack of guidance in terms of moving from theory to application in practice (Maak & Pless, 2006a, 2006b; Voegtlin, 2015).

Within our study, we found evidence that responsible leadership plays a significant role in the practical context of managing complex and ambiguous projects. In particular, we have demonstrated that extensive stakeholder engagement plays a significant role in contributing to handling ethical issues and dilemmas.

Contributions to Practice

Given the paucity of empirical research in the area of ethical decision making and responsible leadership, the findings from this study will have implications for leadership in projects and more widely. The outcomes of this research will enable PMI to consider in what ways ethical standards of practice meet the requirements for project management practice. Furthermore, the findings can inform the development of project managers by providing input that can develop project managers' awareness of how context and moral intensity might influence the decisions they make on projects.

The significance of a sensemaking approach to ethical decision making provides a basis for developing project managers' understanding of the sensemaking processes, thus enhancing their understanding of approaches to handling ethical dilemmas and decision making.

Limitations

As with any research, this study is subject to a number of limitations. First, it is a phenomenological case study and, thus, the findings cannot be widely generalized to different settings or contexts (Yin, 2003). Given the particularly strong culture of this organization, with a core service to client (member) value, this could be an important limitation to bear in mind. It would be useful to replicate the study in different organizational contexts in order to establish the broader applicability of the findings. However, the limitation may be somewhat ameliorated by the fact that the results of the study were supported by arguments and findings from within the extant literature (Yin, 2003). Second, the projects explored had not all reached conclusion and we were, therefore, unable to establish how the approaches to responsible leadership and ethical decision making encountered ultimately impacted the project outcomes. Finally, we did not obtain any input from stakeholders beyond those involved directly in the project. Future research that explores the issues including broader stakeholder perspectives would prove to be particularly valuable.

Tables

Table 1: The Alpha project: Initial codes and higher thematic categories.

Code	Category	Time	Illustrative quote segment
Project Goals	Sustainability	1	Whereas Alpha is very much about efficiency, driving change, but it's also about bringing new, just bringing the life business into the 21st century (CSE[1])
Shared Goals	Shared Mental Models	1	We've all got that agreement to that common goal with an overarching view of what that's going to look like (DSM[2])
Adverse to Risk	Organizational Culture	1	[The organization] is quite, it doesn't like taking risks, so spending that time to document what we currently do today (CSE)
Project Team Characteristics	Selection	1	Yes, but they don't have the emotional resilience and the commitment to the cause so that's why it's difficult because they don't believe it (PM[3])
Project Status	Selection	1	But getting the right people on that small team was really important and the right people weren't necessarily the people that were offered up and I think that was a key piece (DSM)
Location	Confidentiality	1	We are actually off site . . . a few miles out and we are there as a collective group so things are up on the walls, things are, you know, you can say something and it's not, oh, I wonder who has heard this because there are quite sensitive things (CSE)
Stakeholder Mapping	Stakeholder Management	1	We did a stakeholder map of all the people that we thought would be important and why, where we thought they were in terms of their influence and their positivity or their expertise (DSM)
Disclosure	Communication	1	I guess we've tried to go out with as much as we can; we're not telling any lies to anybody, however; I guess at this point in time we haven't done that (CSE)
Previous Projects	History	1	[The organization] invested an awful lot of millions into the first program of work and it didn't really deliver what it was intended to do and they've gone and invested a whole lot more millions into this one (DSM)
Accountability	Decision Making	2	All of the steering group, it's quite small, and we've added in one other director just recently on the HR front, but so far all of that has meant that we've got real momentum and people have taken accountability actually, which is good (DSM)

(continued)

Table 1: The Alpha project: Initial codes and higher thematic categories. *(continued)*

Code	Category	Time	Illustrative quote segment
Restructuring	Rationalization	2	The change process to me is what I do and that's absolutely fine, but when these are people's jobs at potential risk and we don't quite know yet what the structures are, they haven't been signed off (CSE)
Restructuring	Staff Impact	2	At times, I can unleash all that feeling and how does that work, what does that really mean, and it is the really blunt questions as to so, is it that person that goes or is it the role that's going (CSE)
Communication	Trigger Event	2	We had an incident last week where you could say it was a bit of a shambles; the comms still can't come out (CSE)
Anxiety	Emotional Response	2	So whatever I might know going forward on things almost has to just be a different [person] in a different time zone (CSE)
Justification	Rationalization	2	Actually, I'd like to think that I got quite a lot of credibility to be on the program so people will look at it and go, actually there's no selfishness, there's no self-gain, there's no power on this, this is purely factual information based on what we know (CSE)
Project Team	Selection	2	[The project manager's] stance was, I don't want anybody from program management, I don't want any business analysts, all I want is subject matter experts; hence, the makeup of the core design team (CSE)
Strategic Planning	Stakeholder Management	3	And I think we've got to a very clear path forward, which everyone has agreed as a sensible way forward, which is no trivial position to get to where you've managed to get every board member and every nonexecutive director and key stakeholders across the business clear on the direction of travel (SAD[4])
Project Goals	Disclosure	3	I guess the business aren't aware of what the Alpha deliverables are yet, so we've just teamed it under this efficiency banner and said actually it's just good housekeeping (CSE)
Communication	Communication	3	I think that's still up for debate as to whether that's a full hit, here's the 20-odd things that we're going to do or whether it's more of a drip feed almost a timeliness of it (CSE)
Project Team Characteristics	Teamwork	2	Establishment of these core people dedicated for this pretty much meant that we all pulled together on it. It's probably one of the first times I think in a project where people just went, I'll do anything (CSE)
Project Team Characteristics	External Consultant	3	And I think one of the foundational points was we brought in experience, people who had done this before who know this stuff and had depth of experience that's very comforting (SAD)
Change Driver	Sustainability	3	If you look at where we currently were and, indeed, if we don't execute the Alpha business case, the current position deteriorates quite rapidly and you end up with a burning platform (SAD)
Project Progress	Staff Impact	3	We have a rough estimate and that's really rough; I wouldn't say so much on the people side of it, but in terms of the projections, the sales, and volumes and things like that, we've had to make those projections (CSE)

(continued)

Table 1:   The Alpha project: Initial codes and higher thematic categories. *(continued)*

Code	Category	Time	Illustrative quote segment
Restructuring	Staff Impact	3	Life services over the past few years have experienced quite a high volume of that natural attrition and we've played on it in that we haven't recruited to replace it because I guess we could foresee what was coming (CSE)
Values	Organizational Culture	4	It's taken years and years to develop and that is the differentiator, so when our customers deal with us as an organization, they speak to people who are incredibly skilled and caring about their situations and they deal with it in, without doubt, the best way in the insurance industry that I've ever seen (SAD)
Politics	Stakeholder Management	4	You spend a period of time formulating requirements; you then bring those back to the steering group regularly for agreement so every member of the steering group has been individually taken through vast stages of the requirements gathering process to make sure that proposition is fulfilled by the requirements (SAD)
Restructuring	Sustainability	4	When the Alpha business case was put together, and I guess where you number crunch and you do all that stuff, it was quite evident that life services had too many people to sustain it (CSE)
Ethics	Ethical Awareness	4	The only other ethical challenge that we had is one that's dealt with through a lot of the governance committees around the investment, the life business is largely made by the with profits fund, which needs to deliver a good return to members of the profits fund (SAD)
Restructuring	Staff Impact	4	Obviously, as a result of some of those process improvements which we've had done under the Alpha program, we've put in place a load of efficiencies into the life service thing and, as a result of that, some of those people lost their jobs (SAD)
Disclosure	Communication	4	We've left it at that at the moment because what we haven't completely disclosed yet is that actually our business, probably 50% of it, will never come via us going forward because it would just go directly on to the wrap platform (CSE)
Anxiety	Emotional Response	4	So unfortunately, they've seen things evolve in front of their eyes and they haven't actually been a part of it, which is kind of difficult emotionally (CSE)
Project Structure	Decision Making	4	I think the lesson that we've learned is to create a smaller team of people who know exactly what they are doing and hold them to account for it and get out of their way (SAD)
Project Processes	Decision Making	4	There is a delta between the way that the consultants that we've brought in run their projects and our standard project framework, and that has been an interesting dilemma for our project and auditing team (SAD)
Information Sharing	Shared Mental Models	4	We all know what's going on because it's so small still that every week when we give our updates everyone is on the same page as to where things are at (CSE)
Values	Organizational Culture	4	The organization is also known as a very customer-orientated company to do business with and it very much is; it's just, I guess, it hasn't quite worked like that in reality on things so I guess that's the bit that we're trying to change now (CSE)

CSE[1] - Customer Services Expert, DSM[2] - Director of Strategy & Marketing, PM[3] - Project Manager, SAD[4] - Sales Director

Table 2: The Beta project: Initial codes and higher thematic categories.

Code	Overarching Theme	Illustrative Quotations
Lobby	Stakeholder Engagement	We would have got round and seen every individual member of those groups to talk them through what we are doing, where we are at, why we are doing it (PD[1])
Alignment		To actually truly engage people, you've then got to really understand what it is you are trying to do and why you are trying to do it, so the way we've tried to come about that is, actually, we've defined what we are calling the problem statement the reason why we are doing this and actually trying to create a platform (PS[2])
Influence		We've been around all the key members in advance and nobody has got any issues, so something may arise tomorrow and I'll touch wood (PS)
Educate		I suppose the education comes around being able to give them an informed vision or insight into how price operates currently and where we want to take it (PTM[3])
Persuade		I think there was a confidence build rather than anything else; we knew we'd done the work, it was just influencing the people, small meetings like this (PTM)
Slow	Decision Making	Eventually we got the answer; well, we got a partial answer (PTM)
Detail		Everything gets scrutinized. So there's quite a lot of that little bit of inertia (PD)
Consensus		Steering meetings are for making decisions, and what then tends to happen is, as a collective, we don't make decisions and part of some of that kind of behavior (PS)
Confidence		So that kind of confidence thing that we built up and that kind of pre-work that we do, as you say talking to people, now means that we get decisions we need more quickly (PD)
Vision	Leadership	That's changed our vision on how we would tackle growth of policies over profitability and hold our values to the very core of the program (PS)
Openness		I think because we have got very good open communication channels, which is part of the leadership piece, that we're in a good place (PD)
Freedom to Act		If it's someone's idea, we'll just run with it (PD)
Devolve Accountability		Making it very clear and giving people the information to make the strategic decisions has meant that people haven't become frustrated, they understand that pitch and they understand what they need to do (PTM)
Confront Issues		I think my first couple of months on Beta I was questioning the direction of the strategy and I disagreed a lot on what we were planning on doing and raised this (PTM)

(continued)

Table 2: The Beta project: Initial codes and higher thematic categories. *(continued)*

Code	Overarching Theme	Illustrative Quotations
Involve		We've sat down and got to a good conclusion really over what we can achieve and what we can't achieve, come to a pragmatic solution as it were (PTM)
Anticipate	Conflict	I think sometimes if you diffuse a situation and it never comes to a conflict, you forget to mention it, but I think they are situations defused in advance of the conflict becoming just this is going to be an awful conversation (PS)
Escalate		From that point forward, I stepped back from discussions and escalated it to an executive management to determine exactly where resource would be allocated to (PD)
Engage	Team Development	We would have got round and seen every individual team member to engage them with what we are doing, where we are at, why we are doing it (PS)
Purpose		So, fair and accurate prices is a lovely thing to work with. So PIP is here to deliver fair and accurate prices for our members and potential members and the routes of what we are doing with price go to the very heart of who we are as a mutual (PTM)
Expectations		Leadership quite well set out the direction of travel and made it very clear what our objectives are in 2016 (PTM)
Roles		Making it very clear and giving people the information to fulfill the role that they need to play and to make their contribution (PS)
Goals		Having the leadership team spell out to us what our number-one priority is has been useful in terms of planning for what we need to do this year (PTM)
Respect	Values	I'm trying to tread the path that gives what we need—we don't compromise on outcome at all, but treat differing views with respect (PS)
Passion		I'm willing to be passionate and actually call things out (PTM)
Commitment		People are wanting to be part of this and I think people are starting to recognize that actually this is going to be the new way we do stuff, so I think that's generally really positive (PS)
Consensus	Culture	It's been annoying for me, at times, to hear my voice pop up and the executive team need to take time to explore the point until they can arrive at a consensus (PS)
Hierarchical		But it's not my job; I need to know my place (PTM)
Paternalistic		So, we'll all be looked after, we'll all be found homes, and this new thing, it will just be a new structure that if we need to get some retraining and whatever it will just happen (PD)

(continued)

Table 2: The Beta project: Initial codes and higher thematic categories. *(continued)*

Code	Overarching Theme	Illustrative Quotations
Sleepy		I think that the organization is "too nice" . . . it needs to wake up and sharpen up. If it does that, it has a lot of potential (PD)
Risk Averse		Everything gets scrutinized. So there's quite a lot of that little bit of inertia . . . there is a real worry about doing risky things (PS)
Slow		We just need to find ways to break through from the nitty-gritty mass and bring alive the concepts that we are nurturing (PTM)
Lack Challenge		I think we do have a very static culture of not liking change challenge. We don't move in any direction; we don't change tack (PS)

PD[1] - Project Director, PS[2] - Project Sponsor, PTM[3] - Project Team Member

Table 3: The Gamma project: Initial codes and higher thematic categories.

Code	Theme	Illustrative Quotations
Overlap	Multiple Roles	So, in particular with the business change manager, there's a bit of a crossover in responsibilities in so much as the business change manager is responsible for business change being introduced to the business and my role is looking after a certain part of the business (PA[1])
Goal Conflict		So, as well as being the sponsor for potentially implementing a new counter-fraud systems project, I'm also the sponsor of another project, which is looking at when and how and, indeed, whether we should change our core [system or not] (PS[2])
Prioritizing		So my first consideration was, when I'm performing as the sponsor of this project, I'm not the chief . . . manager; I'm the senior leader of the group, delivering a transversal project for the group. So that's the first mind-set I got myself into (PS)
Balance		I saw my role as sponsor and chair to ensure that everyone got the opportunity to put their best case, but that what we didn't do was end up with a project that was unrealistically trying to meet every possible demand, when it was obvious that if we tried to do that, we wouldn't be successful (PS)
Hierarchy		It's documented, clear, and so if there comes a point as to why haven't you delivered by the end of the year, we can say well actually these are the reasons, this is what we looked at, this is what was discussed that was agreed [upon], and in the end, that's not my responsibility. I used to, it used to be like, I've got to deliver this project, but now I understand that we'll provide the information and there are people accountable and responsible in the project board for that (PM[3])
Boundary		
Threat to Project Plan	Project Change	Flagged up that a piece of work . . . wasn't included . . . now my concern at that point is we're doing well on the project, . . . apart from one small item. . . . All that's blown up again in the last few days from the business area, . . . and that is a dilemma at the moment. I say dilemma, I say this, and it's like dilemma (PM)
Long-Term Benefits		I don't want anything delivered that's not fit for purpose; I would rather wait, hold back . . . it's just trying to understand the short-term benefits and look at them, well, actually, if it's not fit for purpose, you could lose engagement of your staff (PA)
Timeliness		That process has gone through with all the proper signatories and signoff that side, but as the new business change manager came in, it was flagged up that a piece of work that she'd worked on [as part of her business area] role wasn't included (PM)

(continued)

Table 3: The Gamma project: Initial codes and higher thematic categories. *(continued)*

Code	Theme	Illustrative Quotations
Engagement	Stakeholder Management	If we are going to implement a more unified intelligence analysis team, where does it report to within the wider business structure, I had no difficulty at all in saying to the finance director and the customer services director, can I have a meeting with you, please, to talk me through this conundrum and get your view on it so we can make a decision (PS)
Network Relation		I've got a reasonably good network within the business, so if there's an issue that's bothering me about this, I've got folk I can go and talk to, to help work out what the right way of approaching it might be (PS)
Emerging Stakeholders		We've now got a more explicit stakeholder group for the project to pay attention to that they didn't have before (PS)
Transparency	Decision Making	Like a shared confidence of what we're doing because of that transparency, I think everyone is able to see what's happening, what decisions are made, and why everyone is quite confident and because they are confident of the workings of the project they are able to allocate that control and let us have more of a control (PA)
Fact Based		So it's very open so there is no, so people don't start to think there are any agendas or feelings being brought into it; it is, here are the facts, here is my decision and why I've made it because of these facts, and here it is, and it's just a very open, let's discuss, yes, there are risks, yes, there are all these things we can mitigate and we can do this, we can do that. So, it's just being open. So, I don't really have any feelings (PA)
Boundary		What I want them [project team] to do is present to the project board and me, as sponsor, the right answer for the business objectives that [Gamma project] has got. If they then need to be compromised because of some broader strategic prioritization, then they've given me the best information possible to know about the consequences of doing that, but it's at my level and the exec that that choice will be made (PS)
		It's more the project board who made the decision, so it's just in my particular role, it's more making sure they are fully informed of the situation and what the impacts of that decision will be to allow them to then make the correct decision (PA)
Lobbying		I was doing some engagement with them myself as project sponsor behind the scenes because they are people in my peer group as senior leaders within the business, so we were having some conversations about this in the background (PS)
"Doing the Right Thing"		Well, I think mostly it's the value of, it's better to do the right ultimate thing for the business than to operate in a way that makes it look like we're still sticking to an original plan. In the long run, your job is to do the right things for the business, not make yourself look good against the plan that's wrong (PS)

(continued)

Table 3: The Gamma project: Initial codes and higher thematic categories. *(continued)*

Code	Theme	Illustrative Quotations
Open Discussion Proactive Monitoring	Ethical Dilemma	It is very easy to discuss openly the concerns at quite an early stage, so knowing that they may not become a major concern, but if people are aware they can keep an eye out for them so that's not a problem at all (PM) The project manager has done a pretty good job of doing that because he's worked out who he needs to talk to very quickly and then gone off and done that, . . . his skill set is to think ahead and then take action rather than always waiting for permission first (PT)
Escalation		If there is a problem or an issue, the right thing to do is to escalate it even if it's difficult because it helps me think through what the right way of resolving it is (PS)
"Doing the Right Thing"		My feeling was that we were treating this very fairly, my feeling was . . . that I was being a responsible project manager in terms of our project and protecting it. So, I felt I was doing the right thing for the project as, too strong a word, as uncomfortable as I felt having to do that with a member of the team (PM)
Interim Lessons	Lessons Learned	I've just described feedback into how we are going to run the next phase of the project and we are going to be doing that, we talked before about using the lessons learnt as an active tool in project management rather than saving it all to the end (PS)
Preventive Tool		I was looking at the longer-term view. . . . So that was documented and discussed with all the key parties, the sponsor, the senior user that had communicated and lessons were learned from that in terms of the communication and reminders out to everybody (PM)
Openness	Team Dynamic	Within the team, the same things really and honesty, openness, don't want stuff just hidden that people think it's behind people's backs or anything like that, it's not, it's open conversations (PM)
Alignment Empowerment		My role as sponsor isn't to get into the detail on all of that, but it is to just keep asking them to lift their heads up and say are the conclusions you are coming to still aligned with those end state purposes we've got and with the timescales and the budgets we've got (PM)
Integration		So we're actually really strong, we've been really strong, we've just got a little bit of change as somebody comes into a team as you would sort of expect as somebody new comes into a well-formed team (PM) So, we've introduced an additional person into the project to take on the business change manager role. She's somebody who works in my head office claims team, and she's been seconded into the team to help fulfil that. So, we're just bedding that in at the moment (PS)

(continued)

Table 3: The Gamma project: Initial codes and higher thematic categories. *(continued)*

Code	Theme	Illustrative Quotations
Paternalistic	Company Culture	Again, it's part of my role; it's not for the project team to worry about that [referring to the dilemma of changes going on outside the project]. . . . I don't expect the project team to have some schizophrenia over whether to do that or not (PS)
Poor Decision Making		So in my mind, there should be a consequence to make a decision and go, this isn't working, let's get a new business change manager in. . . . But if that doesn't work, we just need to change and make those harsh decisions and, as an organization, we're not good at that so we tend to use the wrong people in the roles for too long and then wonder why we haven't succeeded (PM)
Hierarchical		A merging of three potential areas of issue here which I'm finding a way of overcoming. The first is we can be a bit hierarchical, the second is we can be a bit obsessed with structure governance frameworks, so time scales and reporting methods assume more importance than outcomes and modes of achieving them. The third is that we can be a bit siloed, so I have seen other projects struggle more with every party feels they've done what was on their checklist and they all stand around looking puzzled as to why the car doesn't start or the rocket doesn't launch (PS)
Process Obsession		
Siloes		
Fairness/Inclusivity	Leadership	I saw my role as sponsor and chair to ensure that everyone got the opportunity to put their best case, but that what we didn't do was end up with a project that was unrealistically trying to meet every possible demand (PS)
Integration		
Vision		So that obviously includes, as sponsor, making sure I've worked with the various business, businesses that we're doing the project for, to get a really clear picture of what the end state vision is, what will good look like at the end of the project, what are our, what's our vision of what will be true when we've finished, and what that means in terms of how we'll go about doing things, and what the key components of our delivery will be (PS)
Wide Network		From my level of comfort at operating at that level in terms of the types of decisions that might be involved, and I've got a reasonably good network within the business, so if there's an issue that's bothering me about this, I've got folk I can go and talk to, to help work out what the right way of approaching it might be (PS)
External Engagement		Because also, for me as sponsor, because my day job cuts across quite a number of different disciplines within the group. It's quite easy for me to peer over the top of silos if I need to, and sort things out that way. So, it is helpful to have a sponsor who has got a broad network and a good set of stakeholder management across the different departments if there had been a problem (PS)
Coaching		So, I've had to do a fair amount of reassurance and coaching and agreement with Jason about how we will deal with those kinds of issues. But I don't really see that as a problem, because I see that's the inevitable role of a sponsor (PS)

PA[1] - Project Analyst, PS[2] - Project Sponsor, PM[3] - Project Manager

Table 4: The Delta project: Initial codes and higher thematic categories.

Code	Theme	Illustrative Quotations
Trust Building	Conflict	No two people are the same, are they, so you are always going to have that discussion and people having different views and stuff and quite often people appear to have different views (PM[1])
Robust		We need to make sure that we've got that corporate scale and governance over the solution, but that we can deliver it at a price point that's suitable for those agents operating as quite small independent businesses (PST[2])
Choice		His view is they are the best, why are you bothering with all this selection process, you are wasting time, these would be a good choice and, of course, we've got a conflict with other people saying, yes, but you are too close to them, you can't see the perspective, we don't think they are the best service; in fact, here's one I like (PS[3])
Anticipate		I didn't really want to bring in a third, but felt like if I didn't I was going to lose part of my team and it wasn't worth doing that (PS)
Anticipate		In reality, what you end up with when you are buying something like a phone system is both can do it, so technically there's not really anything between the two (PM)
Control		So, we have that direct conflict almost between project sponsors wanting it done tomorrow and us wanting to make sure we get it right. The thing with contracts is a bit like buying insurance really you don't know whether you've got it right or wrong until you actually have to do something against it, so insurance, you don't know if you've bought the right policy until you claim, with a contract you don't really know if you've got it right until (PM)
Consensus	Culture	Lots of people had different views; even the technical guys couldn't decide which they thought was the best, so that was quite a big dilemma at the time as to how we are going to resolve the many different ways you could connect this equipment (PM)
Risk Averse		This organization isn't somewhere that says you've got it wrong, you are sacked; it's not that sort of organization. . . . I honestly have no idea and why they've got that view, but it is prevalent throughout (PM)
Communication		I'm always keen that everybody has a chance to air their views, that we go through a consultative process, that everybody feels that at least they've had a chance to listen to what's trying to be achieved and have a chance to provide some input (PS)
Decision Avoidance		Sometimes people in this place are scared of that inspection, scared of being asked to account for their choice, so when you feel like that the easiest thing to do is don't make a choice, but it's the worst thing you can do for business (PST)
Inclusiveness		So I'm a firm believer in always being able to trace back any individuals' objectives right through to those highest-level company objectives so that they know that what they are doing that day no matter how mundane or frustrating actually; hopefully it's having an impact on those overall corporate objectives and if it's not, then you can challenge (PST)

(continued)

Table 4:   The Delta project: Initial codes and higher thematic categories. *(continued)*

Code	Theme	Illustrative Quotations
Involvement	Decision Making	So we typically get involved in early stages of pre-project work really, so where businesses have got an idea that needs a business case generating or when we need to do some analysis or some research (PST)
Confidence		If you don't make a decision, you can't be wrong is the view that a lot of people take. So, sometimes we do have to almost back them into a corner to get them to make a decision. . . . This project is slightly different and I think they are actually engaged in making the decision; other ones in the past, I've made the decisions and then they've just agreed with me (PM)
Levels		There is a technical decision, whether it's a time-based thing, can we get such and such done in time for whatever, whether it's have we got enough people to do it and if we haven't, how are we going to resolve. (PM)
Closeness		So, one of the issues is who are we going to choose and are we going to choose our favorite which may not be the right answer for the business? (PS)
Consensus		And we had a team meeting and said, what are we going to do and we suggested you know what we should probably go and get some more partners involved, just widen the long list, because it was clear that two potential suppliers weren't going to offer all the answers we needed (PS)
Delay (Trade-off Speed/Quality)		Because it meant that we weren't going to hit our original deadlines, so we expected that we wanted to choose a partner by the start of this year and it's now going to be the middle of year, so that was disappointing (PS)
Time		Yes, we have to realize that whatever we chose now is likely to be a platform for at least the next three years and also is likely to set some of our future directions (PST)
Fairness		I suppose going through the supplier selection . . . was a tricky one to navigate and we had to do that openly and fairly and we made the decision based on the data and evidence we had available to us working in partnership with the agencies (PST)
Complexity		So, quite a lot has happened in a relatively short period of time and so now we have some issues about how do we deal with that supplier (PM)
Number		Those sort of decisions, we don't actually have that many of those usually (PM)
Automatic		So in the first two seconds, you've made your choice up, you've made your mind up, and the rest of the time you spend is just reinforcing your original choice (PS)
Confidence		Are you worried about making a choice? If you are, then you shouldn't be working here because you are going to have to make a choice and you are going to have to say I make that choice, I make it on a conscious deliberate basis and I stand by it (PST)

(continued)

Table 4: The Delta project: Initial codes and higher thematic categories.
(continued)

Code	Theme	Illustrative Quotations
Slow		If you start talking to yourself like that, there's only one thing you are going to do, which is you are never going to make a choice (PS)
Engagement		Most of the time, what we've tried to do is involve everybody in our decision-making process and then usually bring people together around the table to discuss pros and cons of what we are going to do and then get a consensus decision (PST)
Consensus		What I don't want is to make a decision and then throughout the rollout have some of my key decision makers in that process constantly saying, yes, but it's not the one I would have chosen, so I'll be very careful to get everybody in the room at that final point and look them all in the eye and get their assurance that they will back the decision (PST)
Role	Leadership	The project manager role is really about getting whatever it is the business want transferred into something that can be done and then managing that process (PM)
Risk Management		And that you've identified all the risks that could have an impact on that plan and you've put as many mitigating actions and processes in place to deal with those, that you report regularly and frequently on how the project is progressing against its plan and to its budget and scope (PST)
Change		So, there's a much larger ambition in the business to make change (PS)
Coordination		With all projects, the role of the project manager is to coordinate and make the thing happen; however, I'm not the ultimate decision maker (PM)
Maintaining Commitment		Of course, this project impacts quite a large section of the organization across our agency network, so making sure that the agency network interests and views are represented, so I have regular discussions with those people to make sure that their views and understanding of where the project is going is clearly understood (PST)
Consideration		Sometimes you can't act on it and you have to just say you know what I've listened to your opinions or we've taken that into consideration, but we're not going to do that and here are the reasons (PST)
Trust		It moves our working together to another level where we've developed more trust with each other (SP)
Coordinating		I'm just there to get them to the end point; they're the ones who have to do stuff; for example, we need to have a meeting with one of the suppliers, so we've now selected the supplier so if we're going to have a meeting with that supplier, I have to make sure that everybody can get there, where is it going to be, how long is it going to be, what is the agenda, what are our objectives, etc. (PM)
Lobby		If you are talking to a group, some of them may already understand it and will switch off, whereas some of them won't and will be listening, so it's easier one to one (PM)

(continued)

Table 4: The Delta project: Initial codes and higher thematic categories. *(continued)*

Code	Theme	Illustrative Quotations
Influence	Stakeholder Management	What I am there for is to help set some overall direction, to certainly manage stakeholders that are not directly, so to manage out some of my senior stakeholders to make sure that I'm managing out to all of those that have got a vested interest in delivering this project (PST)
Alignment		So, we've got quite an unusual team there because we have some people from our group program office, we have some people from IT, so we have salaried people, and we have some of our colleagues from the agency network who are not our employees; they are our partners so they own their own businesses (PS)
Lobby		We've kept them onside and talked to them about tactics and negotiation and who we are going to work with. So, we've done a fair bit of stakeholder engagement and mostly on an informal basis (PS)
Consensus		So, making sure that the suppliers understand the scope of what we're delivering so that helps to drive price down somewhat and then on the counter to that making sure that agents recognize that it's got to be compliant (PST)
Widespread		The interesting bit is the fact that we're running it from head office, but we have, as part of our project teams and members of the agency network which we've never done before (PS)
Negotiation		So, what our heads are full of at the moment is all the commercial negotiations (PS)
Persuade		Then I was thinking about, well, what happens if [the old partner] wins and [the new partner] says, well, we didn't get a fair go, they're your partner, they're bound to have won, so how do you deal with the fact that they still look after 100 odd sites of ours at the moment on their older technology? (PS)
Negotiation		We are negotiating the contract, contract runs probably too, I hate to think how many hundreds of pages . . . so quite a complex contract, and we're still negotiating some of the financials, so there's a fair amount of that negotiation going on (PM)
Engagement		My experience is this is partly a diplomacy matter of keeping lots of parties involved and we've done really well to get everyone at the table, so don't lose it in the last quarter (PS)
Persuade		We've got three agency sites that have been live on a pilot since early last year; we've been using testimony from those sites to actually convince the rest of the network that this solution has got significant benefit (PST)
Sharing Information		Maybe say it to them directly one on one rather than in a group. . . . It's not so much the facts can't be shared because the facts are the facts; it's the issue of when those facts are shared (PM)
Alignment		And that you make sure that all the stakeholders and decision makers are informed and available to take decisions and corrective action where need be (PST)

(continued)

Table 4:   The Delta project: Initial codes and higher thematic categories.
(continued)

Code	Theme	Illustrative Quotations
Law	Values	So, from that viewpoint, yes, I wouldn't do anything I wasn't happy with. I certainly wouldn't do anything that was against the law (PM)
People		Now, you could argue that some of that doesn't tie in with our "great place to work" philosophy because, for some individuals, we are saying the job no longer exists or you are going to have to move or we're going to do something different, but for the greater good of the organization (PST)
Confidence		That we're all going to be open about where we're up to, there isn't any behind the scenes dealing or any dark room (PS)
Straightforward		It's pretty much a black-and-white type activity; it's phones so there aren't many moralish ideals to go with a phone; are you going to pay for it or aren't you going to pay for it? (PM)

PM[1] - Project Manager, PST[2] - Project Analyst, PS[3] - Project Sponsor

Appendix

Semi-Structured Interview Schedule

Introduce yourself to the respondent and tell them that we are researching decision-making processes in projects. Assure them that no data will be passed back to the organization and that you will tape the interview, but that data will be anonymized. The interview should last about an hour. You should fix the date of the next meeting three months later at the end of the interview.

Questions

1. Can you tell me about yourself? How long have you been in your current job?
2. As a project manager, can you tell me what you understand your role to be?
3. How well would you say the project is currently progressing?
4. How would you characterize relationships within the project team at the moment?
5. Can you tell me in what ways you have engaged with stakeholders over the past three months and any issues this has raised?
6. Can you tell me about some of the most critical incidents that have taken place on the project in the past three months?
7. What were the key decisions that have had to be made?

8. What was your involvement in the decision-making process and how did you do it?

9. What were you feeling at the time?

10. Have there been any conflicts over the past three months? By that, I mean any differences in relation to the pursuit or achievement of particular goals or differences of opinion in what should be done.

11. Have there been any incidents where you have faced a dilemma in terms of what to do on the project, perhaps because of some uncertainty or constraints? Can you tell me about it? What did you do? What sorts of decisions did you take and what did you do or need in order to take them?

12. In relation to these dilemmas, do you think others would have done the same as you? Why?

13. Did you consider the consequences when considering how to respond to this dilemma? For yourself? Your colleagues? The organization? Are these short- or long-term? How serious would you judge these to be? Do you think how you feel about your relationship with these colleagues or the organization affected this? Can you tell me in what ways?

14. Have you faced similar dilemmas to this before? Did you handle them in the same way? How long do you think you spent figuring out how to deal with this compared to previous times?

15. In what ways would you say your values played a part in how you handled that dilemma? Can you tell me about it?

16. How much control do you think you had over how you handled that situation? What factors can you identify as contributing to your perception of the control you had?

17. How much did organizational or specific pressures associated with the project influence either what happened, what you did, or the decisions that you made?

18. To what extent do you feel able to raise concerns or issues (1) in your project, and (2) in the organization without fear or retaliation?

19. Finally, is there anything you think is important relating to the project that you would like to tell me?

References

Aaltonen, K., & Sivonen, R. (2009). Response strategies to stakeholder pressures in global projects. *International Journal of Project Management, 27*, 131–141.

Amaladoss, M. X., & Manohar, H. L. (2013). Communicating corporate social responsibility—A case of CSR communication in emerging economies. *Corporate Social Responsibility and Environmental Management, 20*, 65–80.

American Psychological Association (APA). (2002). *Ethical principles of psychologists and code of conduct.* Available at http://www.apa.org/ethics/code/

Amirshahi, M., Shirazi, M., & Ghavami, S. (2014, March). The relationship between salespersons' ethical philosophy and their ethical decision-making process. *Asian Journal of Business Ethics, 3*(1), 11–33. DOI 10.1007/s13520-013-0028x

Ashforth, B. E., & Anand, V. (2003). The normalization of corruption in organizations. *Research in Organizational Behavior, 25*, 1–52.

Austin, J. E. (2006). 13 Leadership through social purpose partnering. *Responsible Leadership*, 202.

Bansal P. & Kandola S. (2003, March/April), Corporate Social Responsibility: Why good people behave badly in organizations. *Ivey Business Journal*, University of Western Ontario. Available at http://www.iveybusinessjournal.com/view_article.asp?intArticle_ID=404

Bargh, J. A., & Chartrand, T. L. (1999). The unbearable automaticity of being. *American Psychologist, 54*, 462–479.

Brady, F. N., & Wheeler, G. E. (1996). An empirical study of ethical predispositions. *Journal of Business Ethics, 15*, 927–940.

Bredillet, C. (2014). Ethics in project management: Some Aristotelian insights. *International Journal of Managing Projects in Business, 7*(4), 548–565.

Bredillet, C., Tywoniak, S., & Dwivedula, R. (2015). Reconnecting theory and practice in pluralistic contexts: Issues and Aristotelian considerations. *Project Management Journal, 46*(2), 6–20.

Brien, A. (1998). Professional ethics and the culture of trust. *Journal of Business Communication, 17*, 391–409.

British Psychological Society (BPS). (2009). *Code of ethics and governance.* Available at https://beta.bps.org.uk/sites/beta.bps.org.uk/files/Policy%20-%20Files/Code%20of%20Ethics%20and%20Conduct%20%282009%29.pdf

Burnes, B. (2004). Kurt Lewin and the planned approach to change: A re-appraisal. *Journal of Management Studies, 41*, 977–1002.

Butterfield, L. D., Borgen, W. A., Amundson, N. E., & Malio, A. S. T. (2005). Fifty years of the critical incident technique: 1954–2004 and beyond. *Qualitative Research, 5*(4), 475–497.

Carroll, A. B. (1999). Corporate social responsibility evolution of a definitional construct. *Business & Society, 38*(3), 268–295.

Carroll, A. B., & Shabana, K. M. (2010). The business case for corporate social responsibility: A review of concepts, research, and practice. *International Journal of Management Reviews, 12*, 85–105.

Cialdini, R. B., & Goldstein, N. J. (2004). Social influence: Compliance and conformity. *Annual Review of Psychology, 55*, 591–621.

Ciulla, J. B. (2005). The state of leadership ethics and the work that lies before us. *Business Ethics: A European Review, 14*(4), 323–335.

Cleland, D. I., & Ireland, L. R. (2007). *Project management—Strategic design and implementation* (5th ed.). New York, NY: McGraw-Hill.

Craft, J. L. (2013). A review of the ethical decision making literature: 2004–2011. *Journal of Business Ethics, 117*, 221–259.

Daft, R. L., & Weick, K. E. (1984). Toward a model of organizations as interpretation systems. *Academy of Management Review, 9*, 284–295.

D'Amato, A., & Roome, N. (2009). Toward an integrated model of leadership for corporate responsibility and sustainable development: A process model of corporate responsibility beyond management innovation. *Corporate Governance: The International Journal of Business in Society, 9*(4), 421–434.

De Hoogh, A. H. B., & Den Hartog, D. N. (2008). Ethical and despotic leadership, relationships with leader's social responsibility, top management team effectiveness and subordinates' optimism: A multi-method study. *The Leadership Quarterly, 79*(3), 297–311.

Detert, J. R., Trevino, L. K., & Sweitzer, V. L. (2008). Moral disengagement in ethical decision making: A study of antecedents and outcomes. *Journal of Applied Psychology, 93*, 374–391.

Doh, J. P., & Quigley, N. R. (2014). Responsible leadership and stakeholder management: Influence pathways and organizational outcomes. *The Academy of Management Perspectives, 28*(3), 255–274.

Doh, J. P., & Stumpf, S. A. (Eds.). (2005). *Handbook on responsible leadership and governance in global business.* Cheltenham, England, & Northampton, MA: Edward Elgar.

Doh, J. P., Stumpf, S. A., & Tymon Jr., W. G. (2011). Responsible leadership helps retain talent in India. *Journal of Business Ethics, 98*(1), 85–100.

Douglas, P. C. R., Davidson, A., & Schwartz, B. N. (2001). The effect of organizational culture and ethical orientation on accountants' ethical judgements. *Journal of Business Ethics, 34*, 101–121.

Edvardsson, B., & Roos, I. (2001). Critical incident techniques. Towards a framework for analysing the criticality of critical incidents. *International Journal of Service Industry Management, 12*(3), 251–268.

Elango, B., Paul, K., Kundu, S. K., & Paudel, S. K. (2010). Organizational ethics, individual ethics, and ethical intentions in international decision making. *Journal of Business Ethics, 97*, 543–561.

Eskerod, P., Huemann, M., & Ringhofer, C. (2015). Stakeholder inclusiveness: Enriching project management with general stakeholder theory. *Project Management Journal, 46*(6), 42–53.

Festinger, L. (1957). *A theory of cognitive dissonance.* Palo Alto, CA: Stanford University Press.

Flanagan, J. C. (1954). The critical incident technique. *Psychological Bulletin, 51*(4), 327–358.

Flynn, F. J., & Wiltermuth, S. S. (2010). Who's with me? False consensus, brokerage, and ethical decision-making in organizations. *Academy of Management Journal, 53*, 1074–1089.

Foldy, E. G., Goldman, L., & Ospina, S. (2008). Sensegiving and the role of cognitive shifts in the work of leadership. *The Leadership Quarterly, 19*, 514–529.

Ford, R. C., & Richardson, W. D. (1994). Ethical decision making: A review of the empirical literature. *Journal of Business Ethics, 13*, 205–221.

Forte, A. (2004). Business ethics: A study of the moral reasoning of selected business managers and the influence of organizational ethical climate. *Journal of Business Ethics, 51*, 167–173.

Frame, J. D. (2002). *The new project management—Tools for an age of rapid change, complexity, and other business realities* (2nd ed.). San Francisco, CA: Jossey-Bass.

Freeman, R. E. (1984). *Strategic management—A stakeholder approach.* Boston, MA: Pitman Publishing Inc.

Gardiner, P. (2005). *Project management: A strategic planning approach.* Basingstoke, England: Palgrave Macmillan.

Gareis, R., Huemann, M., Martinuzzi, A., Sedlacko, M., & Weninger, C. (2013). *Project management & sustainable development principles.* Newtown Square, PA: Project Management Institute.

Gaudine, A., & Thorne, L. (2001). Emotion and ethical decision-making in organizations. *Journal of Business Ethics, 31*, 175–187.

Glaser, B. G., & Strauss, A. L. (1967). *The discovery of grounded theory: Strategies for qualitative research.* Chicago, IL: Aldine Publishing Company.

Gray, C. F., & Larson, E. W. (2011). *Project management: The managerial process* (5th ed.). Boston, MA, & London, England: McGraw-Hill.

Groves, C. M., Vance, K. S., & Paik, Y. (2007). Linking linear/ nonlinear thinking style balance and managerial ethical decision making. *Journal of Business Ethics, 80*, 305–325.

Harris Interactive. (2009). Available at http://www.harrisinteractive .com/vault/Harris-Interactive-Poll-Research-FT-2009-Business-leaders-4.pdf

Helgado´ttir, H. (2008). The ethical dimension of project management. *International Journal of Project Management, 26*, 743–748.

Henik, E. (2008). Mad as hell or scared stiff? The effects of value conflict and emotions on potential whistle-blowers. *Journal of Business Ethics, 80*, 111–119.

Higgs, M., & Rowland, D. (2011). What does it take to implement change successfully? A study of the behaviours of successful change leaders. *Journal of Applied Behavioural Science, 47* (3), 309–335.

Hill, C. W., & Jones, T. M. (1992). Stakeholder-agency theory. *Journal of Management Studies, 29*(2), 131–154.

Ho, J. A. (2010). Ethical perception: Are differences between ethnic groups situation dependent? *Business Ethics: A European Review, 19*, 154–182.

Huber, G. P., & Lewis, K. (2010). Cross-understanding: Implications for group cognition and performance. *Academy of Management Review, 35*, 6–26.

Hunt, S. D., & Vitell, S. (1986). A general theory of marketing ethics. *Journal of Macromarketing, 6*, 5–16.

Jepsen, A. L., & Eskerod, P. (2009). Stakeholder analysis in projects: Challenges in using current guidelines in the real world. *International Journal of Project Management, 27*, 335–343.

Jepsen, A. L., & Eskerod, P. (2013). *Project stakeholder management*. Farnham, England: Gower.

Jonasson, H. I., & Ingason, H. T. (2013). *Project ethics*. Farnham, England: Gower.

Jones, T. M. (1991). Ethical decision making by individuals in organizations: An issue-contingent model. *Academy of Management Review, 16*, 366–395.

Kerzner, H. (2013). *Project management: A systems approach to planning, scheduling, and controlling* (11th ed.). Hoboken, NJ: John Wiley & Sons.

Kleim, R. L. (2004). *Leading high performance projects*. Plantation, FL: J. Ross Publishing.

Kohut, G. F., & Corriher, S. E. (1994). The relationship of age, gender, experience, and awareness of written ethics policies to business decision making. *SAM Advanced Management Journal*, 32–39.

Komives, S. R., & Dugan, J. P. (2010). Contemporary leadership theories. *Political and Civic Leadership: A Reference Handbook, 1*, 111–120.

Krebs, D. L., & Denton, K. (2005). Toward a more pragmatic approach to morality: A critical evaluation of Kohlberg's model. *Psychological Review, 112*, 629–649.

Krebs, D. L., Denton, E. A., & Wark, G. (1997). The forms and functions of real-life moral decision-making. *Psychological Review, 112*, 629–649.

Laschinger, C., Brent, A. C., & Classen, S. J. (2015). Environmental and social impact considerations for sustainable project life cycle management in the process industry. *Corporate Social Responsibility and Environmental Management, 12*, 38–54.

Lee, M. R. (2009). E-ethical leadership for virtual project teams. *International Journal of Project Management, 27*, 456–463.

Lock, D. (1987). *Project management handbook*. Aldershot, England: Gower.

Lock, D. (2013). *Project management* (10th ed.). Farnham, England: Gower.

Loe, T. W., Ferrell, L., & Mansfield, P. (2000). A review of empirical studies assessing ethical decision making in business. *Journal of Business Ethics, 25*, 185–204.

Loo, R. (2002). Tackling ethical dilemmas in project management using vignettes. *International Journal of Project Management, 20*, 489–495.

Maak, T. (2007). Responsible leadership, stakeholder engagement, and the emergence of social capital. *Journal of Business Ethics, 74*(4), 329–343.

Maak, T., & Pless, N. M. (2006a). Responsible leadership in a stakeholder society: A relational perspective. *Journal of Business Ethics, 66*(1), 99–115.

Maak, T., & Pless, N. M. (2006b). *Responsible leadership.* London, England: Routledge.

Maitlis, S., & Christianson, M. (2014). Sensemaking in organizations: Taking stock and moving forward. *The Academy of Management Annals, 8*, 57–125.

Matten, D., & Crane, A. (2005). Corporate citizenship: Toward an extended theoretical conceptualization. *Academy of Management Review, 30*(1), 166–179.

Maylor, H. (2010). *Project management* (4th ed.). Harlow, England: Financial Times Prentice Hall.

McDevitt, R., Giapponi, C., & Tromley, C. (2007). A model of ethical decision making: The integration of process and content. *Journal of Business Ethics, 73*, 219–229.

McWilliams, A., & Siegel, D. (2001). Corporate social responsibility: A theory of the firm perspective. *Academy of Management Review, 26*(1), 117–127.

Meredith, J. R., & Mantel, S. J. (2009). *Project management: A managerial approach* (8th ed.). London, England: John Wiley & Sons.

Miles, M. B., & Huberman, A. M. (1994). *Qualitative data analysis.* Thousand Oaks, CA: Sage Publications.

Mishra, P., Dangayach, G. S., & Mittal, M. L. (2011). An ethical approach towards sustainable project success. *Procedia Social and Behavioral Sciences, 25*, 338–344.

Miska, C., Stahl, G. K., & Mendenhall, M. E. (2013). Intercultural competencies as antecedents of responsible global leadership. *European Journal of International Management, 7*(5), 550–569.

Mitchell, R., Agle, B., & Wood, D. (1997). Toward a theory of stakeholder identification and salience: Defining the principle of who and what really counts. *Academy of Management Review, 22*, 853–886.

Müller, R. (2014). Guest editorial. *International Journal of Managing Projects in Business, 7,* 4.

Müller, R., Andersen, E. S., Kvalnes, Ø., Shao, J., Sankaran, S., Turner, J. R., Biesenthal, C., Walker, D. H. T., & Gudergan, S. (2013). The interrelationship of governance, trust, and ethics in temporary organizations. *Project Management Journal, 44*(4), 26–44.

Müller, R., Turner, J. R., Andersen, E. S., Shao, J., & Kvalnes, Ø. (2014). Ethics, trust, and governance in temporary organizations. *Project Management Journal, 45*(4), 39–54.

Mumford, M. D., Connelly, S., Brown, R. P., Murphy, S. T., Hill, J., Antes, A. A., et al. (2008). A sensemaking approach to ethics training for scientists: Preliminary evidence of training effectiveness. *Ethics & Behavior, 18,* 315–339.

Muolo, P., & Padilla, M. (2010). *Chain of blame: How Wall Street caused the mortgage and credit crisis.* Hoboken, NJ: Wiley.

Nicolò, E. (1996). Fundamentals of the total ethical risk analysis method (TERA method) with a study of crucial problems in managing distributed multimedia. *International Journal of Project Management, 14*(3), 153–162.

O'Fallon, M. J., & Butterfield, K. D. (2005). A review of the empirical ethical decision-making literature: 1996–2003. *Journal of Business Ethics, 59,* 375–413.

Park, H., & Stole, L. (2005). A model of socially responsible buying/sourcing decision-making processes. *International Journal of Retail and Distribution Management, 33,* 235–248.

Pearce, C. L., Wassenaar, C. L., & Manz, C. C. (2014). Is shared leadership the key to responsible leadership? *The Academy of Management Perspectives, 28*(3), 275–288.

Peikoff, L. (1991). *Objectivism: The philosophy of Ayn Rand.* New York, NY: Penguin Books (Dutton).

Pettigrew, A. M. (1987). Context and action in the transformation of the firm. *Journal of Management Studies, 24,* 649–670.

Pinto, J. K. (2013). *Project management—Achieving competitive advantage* (3rd ed.). Essex, England: Pearson.

Pless, N. M. (2007). Understanding responsible leadership: Role identity and motivational drivers. *Journal of Business Ethics, 74,* 437–456.

Pless, N. M., & Maak, T. (2011). Responsible leadership: Pathways to the future. *Journal of Business Ethics, 98*(1), 3–13.

Pless, N. M., Maak, T., & Waldman, D. A. (2012). Different approaches toward doing the right thing: Mapping the responsibility orientations of leaders. *The Academy of Management Perspectives, 26*(4), 51–65.

Rest, J. R. (1986). *Moral development: Advances in research and theory.* New York, NY: Praeger.

Ruedy, N. E., & Schweitzer, M. E. (2010). In the moment: The effect of mindfulness on ethical decision making. *Journal of Business Ethics, 95*, 73–87.

Sandberg, J., & Tsoukas, H. (2015). Making sense of the sensemaking perspective: Its constituents, limitations, and opportunities for further development. *Journal of Organizational Behavior, 36*(S1), S6–S32.

Savage, G. T., Timothy, N., Whitehead, C., & Blair, J. D. (1991). Strategies for assessing and managing organization stakeholders. *Academy of Management Executive, 5*(2), 61–73.

Scherer, A. G., & Palazzo, G. (2008). *Handbook of research on global corporate citizenship.* Cheltenham, England: Edward Elgar.

Schwalbe, K. (2011). *Information technology.* Boston, MA: Cengage Learning.

Sears, K., Sears, G., & Clough, R. (2013). *Construction project management: A practical guide to field construction management.* Hoboken, NJ: John Wiley & Sons.

Shafer, W. E., & Simmons, R. S. (2011). Effects of organizational ethical culture on the ethical decisions of tax practitioners in mainland China. *Accounting, Auditing & Accountability Journal, 24*, 647–668.

Simon, H. (1955). A behavioral model of rational choice. *Quarterly Journal of Economics, 69*, 99–118.

Sims, R. L., & Gegez, E. (2004). Attitudes towards business ethics: A five nation comparative study. *Journal of Business Ethics, 50*, 253–262.

Singhapakdi, A., & Vitell, J. (1990). Marketing ethics: Factors influencing perceptions of ethical problems and alternatives. *Journal of Macromarketing,* 47–65.

Smircich, L., & Morgan, G. (1982). Leadership: The management of meaning. *The Journal of Applied Behavioral Science, 18,* 257–273.

Sonenshein, S. (2007). The role of construction, intuition, and justification in responding to ethical issues at work: The sensemaking-intuition model. *Academy of Management Review, 32*(4), 1022–1040.

Steenhaut, S., & Van Kenhove, P. (2006). The mediating role of anticipated guilt in consumer's ethical decision making. *Journal of Business Ethics, 69,* 269–288.

Stenmark, C. K., & Mumford, M. D. (2011). Situational impacts on leader ethical decision-making. *The Leadership Quarterly, 22,* 942–955.

Stone-Johnson, C. (2014). Responsible leadership. *Educational Administration Quarterly, 50*(4), 645–674.

Strauss, A. L., & Corbin, J. (1998). *Basics of qualitative research, grounded theory procedures and techniques.* Thousand Oaks, CA: Sage Publications.

Sweeney, B., Arnold, D., & Pierce, B. (2010). The impact of perceived ethical culture of the firm and demographic variables on auditors' ethical evaluation and intention to act decisions. *Journal of Business Ethics, 93,* 531–551.

Thiel, C. E., Bagdasarov, Z., Harkrider, L., Johnson, J. F., & Mumford, M. D. (2012). Leader ethical decision making in organizations: Strategies for sensemaking. *Journal of Business Ethics, 107,* 49–64.

Turner, R. (2014) *Gower handbook of project management.* Farnham, England: Gower.

Turner, R., Huemann, M., Anbari, F., & Bredillet, C. (2010). *Perspectives on projects.* Oxon, England: Routledge.

Turner, R., Huemann, M., & Keegan, A. (2008). Human resource management in the project-oriented organization: Employee well-being and ethical treatment. *International Journal of Project Management, 26*(5), 577–585.

Van Wee, B. (2012). How suitable is CBA for the ex-ante evaluation of transport project and policies? A discussion from the perspective of ethics. *Transport Policy, 19,* 1–7.

Vitell, S. J., King, R. A., & Singh, J. J. (2013). A special emphasis and look at the emotional side of ethical decision-making. *AMS Review, 3*, 74–85.

Voegtlin, C. (2011). Development of a scale measuring discursive responsible leadership. *Journal of Business Ethics, 98*(1), 57–73.

Voegtlin, C. (2015). What does it mean to be responsible? Addressing the missing responsibility dimension in ethical leadership research. *Leadership*. DOI: 1742715015578936

Voegtlin, C., Patzer, M., & Scherer, A. G. (2012). Responsible leadership in global business: A new approach to leadership and its multi-level outcomes. *Journal of Business Ethics, 105*(1), 1–16.

Waldman, D. A., & Balven, R. M. (2014). Responsible leadership: Theoretical issues and research directions. *The Academy of Management Perspectives, 28*(3), 224–234.

Waldman, D. A. (2011). Moving forward with the concept of responsible leadership: Three caveats to guide theory and research. *Journal of Business Ethics, 98*, 75–83.

Waldman, D. A., & Galvin, B. M. (2008). Alternative perspectives of responsible leadership. *Organizational Dynamics, 57*(4), 327–341.

Waldman, D. A., & Siegel, D. (2008). Defining the socially responsible leader. *The Leadership Quarterly, 79*(1), 117–131.

Walker, D., & Lloyd-Walker, B. (2014). Publishing client-side project management capabilities: Dealing with ethical dilemmas. *International Journal of Managing Projects in Business, 7*(4), 566–589.

Watson, G. W., Berkley, R. A., & Papamarcos, S. D. (2009). Ambiguous allure: The value pragmatics model of ethical decision making. *Business and Society Review, 114*, 1–29.

Weick, K. E. (1995). *Sensemaking in organizations*. Thousand Oaks, CA: Sage Publications.

Woiceshyn, J. (2011). A model for ethical decision making in business: Reasoning, intuition, and rational moral principles. *Journal of Business Ethics, 104*, 311–323.

Wright, J. N. (1997). Time and budget: The twin imperatives of a project sponsor. *International Journal of Project Management, 15*, 181–187.

Yin, R. K. (2003). *Case study research, design and methods* (3rd ed.). London, England: Sage.

Contributors

PROFESSOR NICHOLAS CLARKE is professor of human resource management and organizational behavior at EADA Business School, Barcelona. He teaches and researches in the fields of leadership, learning, and development. He has particular interests in the areas of emotional intelligence and respect, and how these affect leadership, leadership development, and learning. He has published extensively in these areas in a number of journals, including *Leadership Quarterly, The Journal of Business Ethics, Human Resource Management, Human Resource Development Quarterly, Journal of Managerial Psychology*, and the *Project Management Journal*®. He has held visiting professor positions at Pompeu Fabra Business School in Barcelona and Toulouse Business School, and sits on the editorial boards of *Human Resource Development Quarterly* and *Team Performance Management*. His new book, *Relational Leadership: Theory, Practice and Development*, published by Routledge, is due out in spring 2018.

PROFESSOR MALCOLM HIGGS is professor of human resource management and organization behavior within Southampton Business School at the University of Southampton. He was previously the head of the school. Prior to joining Southampton, he held posts at Henley Business School, including academic dean, director of the leadership group, and research director. Before joining Henley, he had a long consulting career with a number of international firms, latterly being a partner with Towers Perrin, responsible for leadership and change. He has published a number of books and more than 100 academic journal papers on topics related to leadership, emotional intelligence, and team behavior. Together with Professor Vic Dulewicz, he is coauthor of psychometric tests relating to emotional intelligence and leadership. He is a chartered psychologist and remains an active consultant. He teaches in the areas of leadership, change, and organizational behavior to post-graduate students, in particular on MBA programs. He is a visiting professor at Erasmus University in Rotterdam and Henley Business School. In addition, he is active in supervising doctoral students and has supervised some 24 through to successful completion. He is a regular speaker at national and international academic and practitioner conferences.

DR. ALESSIA D'AMATO is a lecturer in HRM and organizational behavior at Southampton Business School (United Kingdom). She received her PhD from the University of Bologna (Italy). Prior to joining Southampton University in 2014, she served in both the academic and industry sectors, working in major multinationals as well as leading universities (e.g., London School of Economics). Her research interests are in cross-cultural management and leadership and organizational development, and she has teaching commitments in Europe, Asia, and America. Her work has appeared in a number of peer-reviewed journals, including *Work, Employment and Society, Journal of European Management, Corporate Governance, Journal of Managerial Psychology, European Journal of Work and Organizational Psychology,* and in book series.

DR. RAMESH VAHIDI leads the MSc in project management, and teaches modules on project management. She holds a PhD in project management, an MSc in international project management (Distinction), and an MSc and BSc in industrial engineering. Prior to joining academia, she held project manager, project consultant, project auditor, and senior analyst positions in major projects in different industries. She is actively involved with project management professional bodies. Her main research interests are making critical decisions in projects; contemporary, critical, and soft approaches to project management; curriculum design; and project management education. She has presented, chaired, and reviewed for national and international conferences and grants on project management and technology management.